Elements of

ENC 1101
& ENC 1102

Barclay Barrios, PhD
Amy Letter, MFA

Department of English, Florida Atlantic University

HAYDEN
McNEIL

Hayden-McNeil Sustainability

Hayden-McNeil's standard paper stock uses a minimum of 30% post-consumer waste. We offer higher % options by request, including a 100% recycled stock. Additionally, Hayden-McNeil Custom Digital provides authors with the opportunity to convert print products to a digital format. Hayden-McNeil is part of a larger sustainability initiative through Macmillan Higher Ed. Visit http://sustainability.macmillan.com to learn more.

Printed in the United States of America

10 9 8 7 6 5 4 3 2 1

ISBN 978-0-7380-5839-9

Hayden-McNeil Publishing
14903 Pilot Drive
Plymouth, MI 48170
www.hmpublishing.com

Barrios 5839-9 F13 (ENC 1101/1102)

ACKNOWLEDGEMENTS

The editors of *Elements of ENC 1101 & ENC 1102* are grateful to the following Florida Atlantic University people for their contributions to this edition:

Janelle Garcia
Gabrielle Gutting
Elizabeth Kelly
Fred LaCrone
Rosanne Marquart
Jessica Murray-Cooke
Brian Spears

Barclay Barrios would like to thank, in addition, the members of the Writing Committee—Jeffrey Galin, Joanne Jasin, Jennifer Low, and Daniel Murtaugh—for their support of this project as well as his assistants Mike Shier, Alison Amato, and Mary Ruth Sheffield for all of their hard work in preparing the manuscript.

Amy Letter would also like to thank Brian Spears and Bob the mailman for their ideas and support.

TABLE OF CONTENTS

PRELIMINARIES

Plagiarism: Questions and Answers

What is the plagiarism policy?

Students who plagiarize will receive a grade of "F" for the course and a notation of academic irregularity on their transcripts. On the second occurrence, plagiarism can result in expulsion from the University.

What is the basis of this policy?

The policy is governed by the Florida Administrative Code, a collection of regulations implemented at the state level that govern all institutions of higher learning in Florida. For the full text of this code as it relates to plagiarism, see the University Catalog or simply read it below.

What is plagiarism?

Plagiarism is a form of theft. It means presenting the work of someone else as though it were your own; that is, without properly acknowledging the source. Sources include both published and unpublished material written by anyone else, including other students. If you do not acknowledge the source, you show an intention to deceive. Plagiarism can take several forms:

- If you use someone else's words without enclosing them in quotation marks and identifying the author and work cited, you are plagiarizing.

- If you put someone else's original ideas in your own words without identifying the author and work cited, you are plagiarizing.

- If you present new, unique, or unusual ideas and facts that are not the result of your own investigations or creativity without identifying whose they are, you are plagiarizing.

Some of you may have turned in papers in high school that followed one or more of the practices above, and some of you may even have been encouraged to think that these practices were acceptable. In the world outside of high school and college, however, such practices regularly lead to lawsuits, lost jobs, and permanent disgrace. FAU's responsibility is to prepare you for that world, and so the University takes plagiarism very seriously. *Plagiarism will result in academic failure, and it can result in expulsion.*

What should I do if I'm not sure whether or not to cite something?

If you are uncertain whether you are making the proper use of sources in your papers, do one or both of the following:

- Play it safe, and cite the source even if the ideas you are using may turn out to be common knowledge.

- Consult your instructor (not your friends) in advance.

What does "academic irregularity" mean?

Academic irregularities are defined by Regulation 4.001 of the Honor Code (a subsection of the Florida Administrative Code), which forbids cheating, plagiarism, and "other activities which interfere with the educational mission within the classroom."

It's only plagiarism when you present someone else's whole paper as your own, right?
Wrong: plagiarism includes more than just that. Yes, plagiarism includes submitting an essay that you did not write. It also means taking someone else's essay and "changing" it, then submitting it as your own work. It also means including others' phrase(s), sentence(s), paragraph(s), data, and/or ideas in your work without citing the source, making it appear as though they were your own. No matter the particular form, each case of plagiarism is considered theft. Consequences are severe.

Don't people do this all the time, and doesn't that make it okay?
No. You may have been taught otherwise, but that is no excuse: students are regularly failed and dismissed for plagiarism. Don't become a statistic. Don't plagiarize.

But students usually get away with this, don't they?
Actually, plagiarism is almost always easy to spot. Your teachers are professionally attuned to unexplained inconsistencies of writing style, and they have access to an internet service that can conduct large-scale searches for the sources of suspicious papers.

What if I use language from the assignment prompts?
That is plagiarism; any time you take someone else's words and present them as your own, it's plagiarism.

What if I use a definition from a dictionary without citing it?
That is plagiarism; if you take someone else's definition and present it without quoting and citing the source, it's plagiarism.

What if I take something from Wikipedia? Isn't that for everyone's use?
Stealing from *Wikipedia* is no different than stealing from *The Encyclopedia Brittanica*; if you take someone else's words without quoting and citing, it's plagiarism.

What if I use a Web site to help me write my paper?
If you do not cite the source, it's plagiarism. Keep in mind that your instructors, too, have access to Google and are likely to find the same site you did.

I bought a paper off the Web, so that makes it mine to use, right?
No. If you submit the paper as your own work, it's plagiarism.

But it was just a rough draft of a paper…I can't get in trouble for that, can I?
Any work you submit to your instructor must be yours and yours alone. Drafts, homework assignments, response papers—if you plagiarize any of these in whole or in part, you will fail the course.

But I just had someone "clean up" my sentences for me. That's editing, not plagiarizing, right?
If someone changes your sentences for you, then you are plagiarizing. If you are getting help with a paper, ask someone to mark the confusing or awkward sentences for you, but *change them yourself.*

As an international student, I learned a technique called "pasting," where I build new sentences from sentences I know are correct. That's not plagiarism, is it?
It might be. You should check with your instructor.

I was really pressed for time…I had no choice…can't you forgive me just this once?
The English department has a zero-tolerance approach to plagiarism. If, for *whatever* reason, you feel you need to plagiarize, contact your instructor instead. Ask for an extension, explain the situation, work out an alternative—*but don't plagiarize!*

Are there other options for me, then?
Yes. You can speak with your instructor or attend her or his office hours if you need help, guidance, feedback, or assistance. You can also make an appointment with a writing consultant at UCEW, the University Center for Excellence in Writing (see the information on UCEW later in this textbook). You can even visit the English department to make an appointment with the Director of Writing Programs. There's *always* an alternative to plagiarism.

What are the consequences if I plagiarize and get caught?
You will immediately fail the course in which you plagiarized, and a mark will be placed on your transcript indicating that your failure of this course was due to academic irregularity. FAU's "forgiveness" policy cannot be applied to courses which were failed due to academic irregularity, nor can you withdraw from these courses. If you plagiarize a second time, punishment ranges from suspension to expulsion.

What do I do if I am accused of having academic irregularities?
Your instructor will meet with you first. If there has been some misunderstanding, then it should be resolved at this conference. However, if by the end of that conference your instructor remains convinced that you have plagiarized then she or he will give you written notice of the charges and consequences. Your instructor will provide a copy of that written notice to the Director of Writing Programs, who will notify the registrar.

How can I appeal these charges?
After your instructor has given written notice to you and the Director of Writing Programs, you are entitled to a departmental conference with the chair of the English department. You should contact the English department for the e-mail address of the Director of Writing Programs and e-mail your request for a departmental conference.

What happens at the departmental conference?
You will have a chance to explain yourself at the departmental conference. After the conference, you will receive a written notice of the outcome from the English chair.

What if I still wish to contest the charges?
There are further levels of appeal after the departmental conference. Refer to the excerpt of the Honor Code on the following pages, particularly paragraph 3.

What is SafeAssign?
SafeAssign (http://www.safeassign.com) is a service whose system is designed to prevent plagiarism. FAU currently has a license to use SafeAssign's technology to detect plagiarism. Essays are submitted to SafeAssign and added to their database. Newly-submitted essays are compared to previously-submitted essays and to essays on the internet, to help confirm that the essays are original. Essays which are plagiarized, in whole or in part, are very often discovered this way.

Will my work be submitted to SafeAssign?
Possibly; in any case, you should assume so.

I like reading long regulations written in legalese. Can you help?
Florida Atlantic University

Regulation 4.001 Code of Academic Integrity

(1) Purpose. Students at Florida Atlantic University are expected to maintain the highest ethical standards. Dishonesty is considered a serious breach of these ethical standards, because it interferes with the University mission to provide a high-quality education in which no student enjoys an unfair advantage over any other. Dishonesty is also destructive of the University community, which is grounded in a system of mutual trust and places high value on personal integrity and individual responsibility.

(2) Definitions. The FAU Code of Academic Integrity prohibits dishonesty and requires a faculty member, student, or staff member to notify an instructor when there is reason to believe dishonesty has occurred in a course/program requirement. The instructor must pursue any reasonable allegation, taking action where appropriate. Examples of academic dishonesty include, but are not limited to, the following:

(A) Cheating

1. The unauthorized use of notes, books, electronic devices, or other study aids while taking an examination or working on an assignment.

2. Providing unauthorized assistance to or receiving assistance from another student during an examination or while working on an assignment.

3. Having someone take an exam or complete an assignment in one's place.

4. Securing an exam, receiving an unauthorized copy of an exam, or sharing a copy of an exam.

(B) Plagiarism

1. The presentation of words from any other source or another person as one's own without proper quotation and citation.

2. Putting someone else's ideas or facts into your own words (paraphrasing) without proper citation.

3. Turning in someone else's work as one's own, including the buying and selling of term papers or assignments.

(C) Other Forms of Dishonesty

1. Falsifying or inventing information, data, or citations.

2. Failing to comply with examination regulations or failing to obey the instructions of an examination proctor.

3. Submitting the same paper or assignment, or part thereof, in more than one class without the written consent of both instructors.

4. Any other form of academic cheating, plagiarism, or dishonesty.

(3) Procedures.

(A) If the instructor determines that there is sufficient evidence to believe that a student engaged in dishonesty, the instructor will meet with the student at the earliest possible opportunity and provide notice to the student of the instructor's perception of the facts, the charges against the student, and the sanction. The instructor may not remove the student from the course until the appeal process has come to a conclusion.

(B) If, after this meeting, the instructor continues to believe that the student engaged in dishonesty, the instructor will provide the student written notice of the charges and the penalty. A copy of this statement shall be sent to the chair of the department or director of the school/program administering the course.

(C) The student is entitled to an opportunity to be heard at a meeting with the instructor and chair/director to review and discuss the instructor's charges/statement. Such request for a meeting must be made in writing and received by the chair/director within five (5) business days of receipt of the instructor's charges/statement. The purpose of the meeting is to discuss the facts and to advise the student of the appeal process. The chair/director will provide the student, the instructor, and the dean of the college administering the course a summary of both the student's position and the instructor's position.

(D) The student may appeal in writing to the dean of the college administering the course. The appeal must be received by the dean within five (5) business days of receipt of the chair/director's summary from the review meeting. The dean will convene a Faculty–Student Council ("Council"), which will be composed of the dean (or designee), two faculty members, and two students. The dean (or designee) will act as chair of the Council, direct the hearing, and maintain the minutes and all records of the appeal hearing, which will not be transcribed or recorded. The hearing is an educational activity subject to student privacy laws/regulations, and the strict rules of evidence do not apply. The student may choose to be accompanied by a single advisor, but only the student may speak on her/his own behalf. The student and instructor may present testimony and documents on his/her behalf. Additional witnesses may be permitted to speak at the dean's (or designee's) discretion and only if relevant and helpful to the Council. The Council will deliberate and make a recommendation to the dean to affirm or void the instructor's findings of academic dishonesty. The dean (or designee) will inform the student and instructor in writing of his/her findings of academic dishonesty after receipt of the Council's recommendation.

(E) The student may request an appeal in writing of the dean's findings of academic dishonesty to the University Provost (or designee) and include relevant documentation in support of such appeal. The University Provost (or designee) will notify the student, dean, and instructor of his/her decision in writing. This decision by the Provost (or designee) constitutes final University action.

(F) If there is a finding that the Code of Academic Integrity has been violated, the chair will notify the University Registrar that the following notation be included on both the student's official transcript and on the student's internal record: "Violation of Code of Academic Integrity, University Regulations 4.001." If such violation is appealed and overturned, the dean or University Provost (or their designees) will notify the University Registrar that such notation should be removed from the student's transcript and internal record.

(4) Penalties.

(A) The instructor will determine the penalty to be administered to the student in the course. Penalty grades cannot be removed by drop, withdrawal, or forgiveness policy. Students should be aware that, in some Colleges/programs, failure in a course or a finding of dishonesty may result in other penalties, including expulsion or suspension from the College/program.

(B) In the case of a first offense, the student may elect to complete a peer counseling program administered by the Division of Student Affairs by the end of the semester following the semester in which the dishonesty occurred. Upon successful completion of this program, the notation regarding violation of the Code of Academic Integrity will be expunged from the student's official transcript. The grade, however, will remain unchanged and cannot be removed by drop or forgiveness policy. Also, the notation will remain in internal University student records.

(C) In the case of a repeat offense, even if the notation of violation of the Code of Academic Integrity from the first offense had been expunged from the official transcript as a result of successful completion of the peer counseling program, the student will be expelled from the University.

Specific Authority: Article IX of the Florida Constitution, 1001.706, 1001.74 F.S., Board of Governors Regulations 1.001, 6.010, and 6.0105. History–New 10-1-75, Amended 12-17-78, 3-28-84, Formerly 6C5-4.01, Amended 11-11-87. Formerly 6C5-4.001. Amended 5-26-10.

Write additional questions and answers from class discussion here:

Q:_____

A:_____

_____

_____

_____

Q:_____

A:_____

_____

_____

_____

Q:_____

A:_____

_____

_____

_____

Section 1

By signing this statement, I attest that

- I have read the questions and answers about plagiarism.

- I have had the opportunity to ask my instructor questions about these materials and have had those questions answered to my satisfaction.

- I understand what plagiarism is.

- I understand the consequences of plagiarizing.

Signature:_____

Print name:_____

Date:_____

Absences: Questions and Answers

What is the absence policy?

More than two weeks' worth of unexcused absences may result in an "F" unless you successfully apply for a grade of "W." Our collective experience as teachers of writing suggests that students who miss more than two weeks' worth of class are unable to produce passing work and ultimately fail the class. That fact reflects both the rigorous pace of this course and the fact that what students learn in this class, they learn in the classroom through group work, discussion, and writing activities (work that cannot be made up).

Is that two weeks of absences all at once?

It could be; it could also be any combination of absences spread out over any combination of days or weeks.

But it's only unexcused absences, right?

Absences that are excused for University-approved reasons allow you to make up any work you have missed without direct penalty. However, please keep in mind that it remains true that the more class you miss the less likely you are to produce passing work. While we will not directly penalize you for excused absences, you may miss important classwork that cannot easily be made up.

Then what's the difference between excused and unexcused absences?

You are allowed to make up work that you miss because of an excused absence. Making up work that you miss because of unexcused absence is at your instructor's discretion.

So I'm OK as long as I don't miss that much class, right?

Maybe. Keep in mind that your instructor may lower your grade for repeated absences. If your work is borderline, you could end up failing the class from having your grade lowered by multiple absences.

I switched into this section late in the drop/add period so I missed the first couple of classes. Do those missed classes count?

That depends on the particular situation, so you should be sure to discuss this with your instructor as soon as possible—and without disrupting the class. These absences may indeed be counted toward your total. Since the absence policy is largely about being *in* the class—in its dynamics, in its small groups, in its workshopping—every time you are not in the classroom you are functionally absent. Even if you were attending another section, you were not contributing to the class dynamic of your current section.

My schedule is so tight because of work (or other classes) that it's very hard for me to make it to class on time. Being tardy doesn't count when it's not my fault, does it?

It might. Your instructor will provide you with specific guidelines on how tardiness will be handled in your particular section. If she or he does not, ask. You might want to consider moving to a different section, one that fits more comfortably within your schedule. Otherwise, you will want to alert your instructor to this problem, ask what accommodations might be made, do your best to arrive on time, and enter the classroom quietly when you are late.

What if I am sick?

The policy was created to allow for circumstances beyond your control, including illness. If you miss more than two weeks of class due to illness, you should probably speak to your academic advisor about the possibility of a medical withdrawal.

What is a medical withdrawal?

According to the University Catalog, a medical withdrawal applies to students who wish to withdraw "from ALL classes in the current semester due to exceptional circumstances, such as illness of the student, military conscription, call to active duty, or death of an immediate family member (parent, spouse, child, sibling, or grandparent)." Students who qualify for a medical withdrawal (or "Exceptional Circumstances Withdrawal") may, according to the University Catalog, "receive a full refund, less non-refundable fees." Contact the Dean of Student Affairs about Exceptional Circumstances Withdrawals.

What if I am on a sports team? What if I have to miss for some other University-approved reason?

As soon as you know your travel schedule, check it against your class schedule. If you are going to miss more than two weeks' worth of classes, speak with your instructor immediately. You may have to move to another section. It is your responsibility to notify your instructor of these absences ahead of time, and your responsibility to make up any work you miss.

What if I have to miss class due to religious observances?

You should alert your instructor at the very start of the semester if you will be missing class for religious observances. You will want to remind your instructor just before the absence, you will want to have formed a plan with your instructor on how you might make up any missed work, and you will want to make sure that your attendance is otherwise regular.

Does this mean attendance counts more than the work I do?

The two are closely linked. Gordon Rule courses are workshop courses. In content-based courses, such as Biology, your grade is determined by your mastery of the content, through quizzes, tests, and exams. If you miss a number of these classes, you can recover by learning the material on your own. However, in a workshop-based course, what you learn (more than anything) is process. That process is practiced and modeled in the classroom, in drafting, in group work, in peer revision. If you are not present in the classroom, then you are not taking part in the process it is your responsibility to learn.

Why two weeks, though? Isn't that arbitrary?

No. It's best to think of this in terms of human law and natural law. Human laws are the ones we decide upon as a society and therefore are somewhat arbitrary. For example, it's illegal to drive on the left side of the road here but not in England. Natural laws, on the other hand, are self-enforcing: if you step off a building you will fall. Similarly, experience has shown that students who miss two weeks or more of writing classes miss so much of the learning of the class that their work is severely jeopardized. That is, if you're missing this much class the chances of producing passing work are greatly reduced. In this sense, our position on absences is more a warning than a proscription: if you miss that much class, it's highly likely you will fail with or without the policy.

Are there exceptions to this policy?

Rarely. Speak with your instructor—who might, in turn, consult with the Director of Writing Programs. However, it remains your responsibility to be proactive in these matters. Exceptions are more likely to be made with students who have made all reasonable efforts to attend class, who have handed in work on time and have participated in class, and who speak with their instructor before excessive absences have accumulated.

Write additional questions and answers from class discussion here:

Q:_____

A:_____

_____

_____

_____

Q:_____

A:_____

_____

_____

_____

Q:_____

A:_____

_____

_____

_____

By signing this statement, I attest that

- I have read the questions and answers about absences.

- I have had the opportunity to ask my instructor questions about these materials and have had those questions answered to my satisfaction.

- I understand the importance of attendance.

- I understand that it is my responsibility to alert my instructor to, and to make up work missed because of, excused absences.

- I understand that I may fail this class based on poor attendance.

Signature:_____

Print name:_____

Date:_____

Permission to Use Your Work

Please read the following, check the appropriate box, and sign this form.

❏ I, the undersigned student, AGREE to allow my instructor to reproduce my work anonymously, in whole or in part, for pedagogical or scholarly purposes. I further understand that this permission to use my work will not impact my grade in any way.

I understand that if my work is quoted for publication, my instructor will make every reasonable effort to contact me in advance to discuss proposed uses and to provide me with a published copy of the full text.

❏ I, the undersigned student, DO NOT agree to allow my instructor to reproduce my work, in whole or in part, for pedagogical or scholarly purposes outside the classroom. I further understand that this refusal to use my work outside the classroom will not impact my grade in any way.

Signature:_____

Print name:_____

Date:_____

GRADING CRITERIA

Grading Criteria

These grading criteria began as a wiki-powered project driven by the teachers of our program. They have been refined by the Writing Committee and adopted by the faculty of the department of English. Papers are evaluated in five categories: thesis/argument/reasoning, evidence/quotation/support, organization, audience, and grammar/language/formatting.

Plagiarism and Academic Irregularity

Issues of academic irregularity such as plagiarism supersede these criteria; any work that has been plagiarized in whole or in part will result in a failing grade for the course as a whole and a notation of academic irregularity on the student's transcript. Please refer either to the FAQs on plagiarism in this text or to the University Honor Code contained in the University Catalog.

The criteria are:

Not Passing

Note: Papers that are not passing may exhibit many of the characteristics described by the criteria below. However, papers that have any one of the following elements cannot pass: no argument, no attention to the assignment, or egregious error to the degree that meaning is severely impeded.

Thesis/Argument/Reasoning

Not Passing papers have little or no sense of argument, thesis, position, or purpose, thus suggesting that the student is unable to think critically in relation to the readings or unable to reproduce that critical thinking in writing. Specifically:

- The paper does not address the prompt

- The paper contains no clear argument

- The paper contains a narrative instead of expository essay

Evidence/Quotation/Support

Not Passing papers generally avoid close engagement with the readings; what engagement there is might suggest significant misreading. In other words, the use of text suggests that the student is unable to read critically or unable to connect critical reading to independent and original thinking. Specifically:

- The paper includes no textual support, no quotation at all

- The paper includes textual support, but indicates a misreading or haphazard reading of the text

- The paper includes quotation or summary but fails to use it to support any argument

- The paper has so many quotations that it seems the student is using quotation and summary to "write" the paper instead of providing his or her own analysis

- When research is required, the sources may be inappropriate for the assignment, non-scholarly when scholarly sources are required, or contradictory within the context of the paper.

Organization

Not Passing papers often have serious problems with organization, reflected either in a failure to meet minimum requirements for length or in a level of disconnection that hinders the comprehension of the reader. Specifically:

• The paper is not sufficiently developed and often will therefore not meet minimum length requirements

• In the paper, there is no clear relationship between the paragraphs, the ideas expressed, the quotations used, or the summaries presented

• The paper has no clear pattern of organization, thus impeding meaning and comprehension

Audience
• The paper adopts an inappropriate tone by using slang, informal English, or nonacademic prose

• The paper shows little or no awareness of the reader's need for contextual information

Grammar/Language/Formatting

Not Passing papers pay little attention to issues of grammar, language, and presentation. At times, this will reflect serious language concerns in a student; however, it may also reflect severe carelessness on the part of the student. Specifically:

• The paper contains grammatical errors that impede meaning, including repeated significant errors (subject/verb agreement, sentence boundary issues) and/or convoluted syntax that makes it difficult to understand what the student is trying to say

• The paper shows that the student made little or no attempt to conform to MLA rules of documentation

C Range (C or C+)
Note: C- papers are not passing; however, the use of C- is often intended to indicate that a student has progressed significantly or is producing work that is almost but not quite passing.

Thesis/Argument/Reasoning

"C" or "C+" papers show that the student can articulate a position in relation to a set of readings. That articulation—which we might variously call the paper's argument, thesis, or project—represents the start of critical thinking. Specifically:

• The paper addresses the prompt

• The paper has an argument, even though that argument may not be stated in the introduction or may not ever be stated clearly

• In C+ papers, the argument is stated clearly but reflects only what was discussed in class, thus showing no original thought

Evidence/Quotation/Support

"C" or "C+" papers demonstrate that students are acquiring skills with critical reading, reflected through their ability to work with texts in support of their position. Specifically:

- The paper has quotations that relate to the topic and argument, but the relationship is often not explained

- Particularly for low-level C papers, the paper has some quotations that do not support (and may even contradict) the assertions made in the paper

- Particularly for C+ papers, the paper has original ideas, but these ideas tend to be dropped or repeated rather than developed

- In assignments that ask students to work with more than one text, the paper provides quotations from all required texts, but uses them in isolation, hence weakening the connection between the ideas of those two authors

- When research is required, the sources used are mostly appropriate for the assignment and/or scholarly, but they may result in repetition of facts and ideas within the paper rather than depth of thought or variety of perspective.

Organization

"C" or "C+" papers have a basic sense of organization; that is, the student substantially controls the shape of the paper, though some areas may interrupt the flow of the paper. Specifically:

- The paper includes leaps in logic and expects readers to follow implicit patterns of thought

- The paper may have some paragraphs that include unrelated ideas and lose argumentative focus

- The paper offers no link between the ideas expressed in each individual paragraph; transitions between paragraphs are non-existent or forced

- The introduction and conclusion are often formulaic; that is they do not seem uniquely connected to the body paragraphs

- Particularly in C+ papers, the order of some paragraphs could be changed without changing what the paper is saying

Audience
- The paper adopts an appropriate tone, but may sometimes lapse into slang, informal English, or nonacademic prose

- The paper shows some awareness of the reader's need for contextual information

Grammar/Language/Presentation

"C" or "C+" papers reflect less skill with language and presentation. Though errors remain, there is clear evidence that the student is working to improve these issues. Specifically:

• The paper may show patterns of error, but these errors generally do not impede meaning; they may instead represent errors such as article usage, punctuation, or missing words

• The paper attempts to follow rules of MLA documentation, but errors or omissions are evident

B Range (B-, B, B+)

B-, B, B+ papers have all the elements of papers in the "C" range and have most of these additional elements as well.

Thesis/Argument/Reasoning

"B-," "B," and "B+" papers show the student performing solid and original critical thinking, reflected in a clearly stated position (argument, thesis, project) that is in some way original, moving beyond class discussion. Specifically:

• The paper has an argument that shows some originality by expressing ideas that were not expressed in class

• The paper's purpose is clearly, authoritatively stated from the beginning; that is, it is possible to identify a sentence or group of sentences that contain the purpose or project of the paper

• The paper has an argument that moves beyond what the readings have said while also clearly engaging with the readings

• The paper has an argument that avoids absolute claims (with terms like "all," "never," "always") and that acknowledges its limits

• B+ papers tend to have particularly original, thoughtful, or authoritative arguments

Evidence/Quotation/Support

"B-," "B," and "B+" papers demonstrate that the student is increasingly comfortable with the text, as shown by an ability to use close textual engagement in support of the argument; B+ papers, in addition, show a kind of authority in relation to the text or a particularly original or insightful reading. Specifically:

• For B- papers, the paper has clear connections between two or more texts, but more development may be needed to show how those connections support the argument

• Although all paragraphs provide support for the argument, they still include more summary of the text than analysis

- The paper contains quotations that clearly support the argument, and the student is able to explain how those quotations provide that support; however, the use of quotation and accompanying explanation may be repetitive throughout the paper

- Quotation is used in a way that demonstrates thorough understanding of text

- The paper may, however, avoid possible counter-arguments; portions of the texts that may not support (or may completely go against) the argument are avoided

- When research is required, the sources are strong and varied in relation to the requirements of the assignment. Their use in the paper displays depth of thought, including a diversity of perspectives about the topic, which may include counter arguments as appropriate. However, the incorporation of the outside information may lack cohesion with the paper's argument or purpose.

Organization

"B-," "B," and "B+" papers have solid organization. That is, there is a clear order to the paper even if some transitions are rough or missing. B+ papers tend to have an especially strong, fluid, or complex organization that may fall short in one or two moments. Specifically:

- The paper's paragraphs follow a logical order, building on each other as the argument unfolds

- There is an attempt made at transitions between paragraphs, even if some of these transitions are rough, awkward, or implicit

- The introduction clearly sets forth what the body paragraphs will accomplish

- The conclusion states the implications of what the body paragraphs have accomplished (answers the question "so what?"), though it may lapse into partial restatement of the introduction

Audience
- The paper adopts an appropriate tone by avoiding slang, informal English, or nonacademic prose

- The paper shows a consistent awareness of contextual information needed by readers both inside and outside the class

Grammar/Language/Formatting

"B-," "B," and "B+" papers show the student attaining increased control over problems of presentation and language. Specifically:

- There is clear evidence that the paper has been proofread and that patterns of error have been addressed, resulting in infrequent error (typographical or grammatical)

- Paper adheres to MLA style and quotations are properly documented

A Range (A-,A)

"A-" and "A" papers have all the elements of papers in the "B" range and have these additional elements as well.

Thesis/Argument/Reasoning

"A-" and "A" papers demonstrate strong critical thinking. The student is able to respond to the readings and to the assignment with originality and authority. Specifically:

- The paper presents an original and compelling argument that addresses the prompt fully and avoids absolute claims

- The argument is aware of its underlying assumptions and acknowledges its limits

- The argument is stated with such authority that the order of its statements and the linkages between them seem inevitable

Evidence/Quotation/Support

"A-" and "A" papers reflect the student's depth of critical reading. Rather than being subject to the texts and their authors, the student begins to assume more and more authority in relation to these texts, both through insightful analysis and through deft use of quotation in support of the argument. Specifically:

- The paper works closely with quotation in multiple ways; it connects quotations from different essays within a paragraph in unique and fluid ways and/or returns to the language of a quotation in the analysis of another quotation or reading

- Quotations are introduced, discussed, clearly related to the argument, and properly cited

- Quotations are incorporated seamlessly into grammatically correct sentences (that is, the sentence that includes a quotation works grammatically even with the quotation marks removed)

- The paper considers and responds to possible counter-arguments

- When research is required, the sources used are strongly fitting in relation to the assignment and the paper's purpose. Their use in the paper displays depth of thought, including a diversity of perspectives about the topic, which may include counter arguments as appropriate. The sources are seamlessly incorporated, adding nuance to the paper without distracting from the paper's unique argument.

Organization
- Paragraphs contain well-developed subtopics; they have enough information to stand alone but also relate to each other in that they all support the argument

- Transitions between paragraphs are not forced or confusing. The next paragraph always seems like the next logical step to take to support the argument

- Conclusion draws from the main ideas of the essay and opens up new ideas for further research/development

Audience
- The paper inspires confidence in the audience, addresses significant issues, and leaves the reader with the sense of having learned something

- The paper anticipates the audience's questions and needs for contextual information

Grammar/Language/Presentation
- The paper is virtually free of grammatical and typographical errors

- The paper adheres to MLA style

THESIS/ARGUMENT/REASONING

Introduction to Argument

In order to write a compelling essay, you must have an *argument*. This basic checklist will help you to build a strong argument.

- To help you find an argument for a paper, list all possible connections you can make between the essays. Then try to find a pattern in those connections.

- Clearly state what you want to argue before you start arguing it.

- Give evidence to support what you're arguing.

- Elaborate on the evidence—don't try to let it "stand alone."

- Be specific! Name names! Give details! Be specific in your argument and your evidence.

- Think through your argument—if there's a gap in your logic, don't ignore it. If there's an exception to a general assertion you've made, point it out!

- Do not attack or insult—show respect, and your writing will be more respectable.

- Organize your ideas and your evidence: have a plan, and make it happen!

- Anticipate objections—and answer any significant objections to your argument before the reader has time to object.

- Don't use evidence that is too brief or too long. Figuring out what is too brief and too long requires good judgment, and it is very important.

- If you get to the end and your argument has changed or shifted, go back to the start of your essay and re-write the initial assertions of your argument to account for the changes.

All About Argument

There are two essential skills to this class, and to all composition classes: connection and argument. And it's not that those are the two random hoops we decided students needed to jump through. Instead, they are the two skills that best reflect critical thinking. And they reflect that thinking in a very particular way. The kind of work we ask you to do is the kind of work we do as academics. This is what all your professors do. We think. We think a lot. We think hard. Then we write about what we think. We write papers, articles, and books that make arguments about issues we care about. We don't expect you to become professors, but we do expect you to have the same kind of thinking abilities, because what you learn here will help you throughout college and beyond.

Name _____

▪ ▪ ▪ **Group Exercise**
Argument Exercises I–VIII

I.   Argument is a kind of conversation

Let's start with the basics. Argument is a kind of conversation, so, as a group, create a definition of conversation. We all know it's a kind of speaking, but what makes a conversation a conversation? Jot some notes here:

OK. Now imagine that each of the essays we read are part of a larger conversation. Thinking about the essays, their themes, their issues and their points, describe the larger conversation of each essay as best you can. What do you think are some of the larger issues? Jot some notes here:

II. There are different kinds of argument

Argument is a kind of conversation, but even within that there are many different kinds of argument. As a group, jot down some of the characteristics of each of the different kinds of arguments. What are they like? How would you be able to tell one from another? Jot notes:

a. an argument between lovers

b. an argument between political candidates

c. an argument in a courtroom

d. a scientific argument

Now, as a group, explain the difference between these two sentences: "They're having an argument" and "You have a convincing argument."

Think about this class. What kind of argument do you think your paper should have? Describe what it's like compared to the examples above.

III. What an argument looks like

Consider the following statements. Which one is an argument, and why?

a. Princeton and FAU are universities.

b. Princeton's writing program is similar to FAU's writing program.

c. Princeton's writing program is similar to FAU's writing program, which means that FAU is as good as an Ivy League school in terms of writing.

IV. Some models for argument in the composition classes

Here are some of the ways we talk to each other about argument. These are all "models" teachers use to describe the kind of work we want students to do:

a. **Framing**: The purpose of the paper is to use the ideas from one essay to "frame" the ideas from the other. That is, you examine the second essay using terms and concepts from the first, as though examining the second essay through a frame or lens provided by the first. For example, using Princeton's program to "frame" FAU's program.

b. **Conversation**: The purpose of the paper is to put the two essays into conversation. That is, you use the ideas and terms and concepts from one essay to discuss or evaluate the ideas from the other. For example, discussing Princeton's and FAU's programs together.

c. **Case/Theory**: The purpose of the paper is to use a theory about something from one essay and to test it using another essay as a particular case. That is, you evaluate how effective the first author's ideas are when applied to a second author. For example, you might examine Princeton's program as a theory of what an effective program should be like and then test it with FAU's.

d. **Application**: The purpose of the paper is to apply the ideas of one essay to the ideas of the other. That is, you take a term or concept and apply it to the new essay, learning something new either about the term or about the new essay. For example, you might apply the ideas of Princeton's program to FAU's.

As a group, discuss these different models, and then jot some notes on what they have in common. Think about what model seems clearest to you, if any. And, as a group, try to come up with an explanation of what an argument should do in a composition paper.

V. Terms for discussing argument

Think about the following descriptions:

a. **And so?**: An argument has to have a point. It has to first assert a connection between the two essays but then also answer the question "and so?" Essay A is like (or unlike) Essay B and so…

b. **Point**: An argument is the point you are trying to make. It is the idea or thought you are trying to get across. A point is something you prove, and a point is also something that we haven't thought of or discussed yet.

c. **Making knowledge**: An argument is a way of making new knowledge. How do we learn something new? We think about what we know and then we come to a conclusion. That conclusion is a new piece of knowledge that we can express. If you just read Essay A you learn X, but after reading Essay B we now learn Y about Essay A. The argument tells us something new, something we haven't thought about before.

Discuss these ideas as a group and jot a few more notes on what you think an argument should do in a composition paper:

VI. OK, but I still can't think of an argument myself. So what do I do?

Well, the first thing to do is to realize a few things. One, you're not expected to fully understand argument now. You will understand, someday, when you are done with writing classes as a whole. You are, however, expected to *begin* understanding argument as you move through your freshman writing courses. Two, it's not easy, and it's not supposed to be. Finding an argument takes a lot of thinking, which, after all, is the whole point. Three, you should now (we hope) have some sense of what an argument does, and that's a good start too.

Here are some tips for finding an argument for your paper:

a. Think about the larger conversation. Both authors are talking about similar things; that's why we can make connections between their essays. But the connections are not just in specific terms or ideas or concepts or quotations. They are also between the larger issues. Start by thinking about what the larger issue is between the essays, and then think about how each of these essays addresses this issue. For example, if the issue is literacy, then what does each author say about literacy, in a larger sense?

b. Think about the connections. Make a list of every connection you see, and then start looking for connections between the connections. Is there a set of connections about one idea? How do those connections relate to each other? To both essays? To larger ideas?

c. Think about what you're trying to prove. It's not enough to prove a connection. Yes, that takes some thinking, but not enough. You have to think about what the connections mean.

d. Think about what we're learning from your paper. What have you discovered by bringing these essays together? Do the ideas of one author extend the ideas of the other author into a whole new area? Are the ideas of one author limited because of what the other author shows?

e. Think about one essay and then the other. Imagine you only read the first essay. Make a list of what you would have believed, thought, or learned. Then, think about how the second essay would change, challenge, or extend that.

VII. Argument worksheet

If you're still stuck, try this worksheet:

The larger issue behind both these essays is _____ .

My first author, _____ , has the following argument about this issue in his/her essay:

My second author, _____ , has the following argument about this issue in his/her essay:

I have located the following connections between these essays:

These connections all have to do with _____ . While _____ says _____ about _____ , (extends/challenges/disproves/modifies) that idea because _____ .

VIII. Testing your argument

Once you think you have an argument, use the following questions to test it and see if it's clear and strong:

a. Do you express it in one sentence? A clear argument should always be identifiable in your paper. Someone should be able to point to a sentence in your introduction and say "Here, this is the argument."

b. Do you express it in terms of both essays? Though this is not always true, a good rule of thumb is that the argument should contain the name of each author. That makes it clear that the heart of the argument is a larger connection.

c. Is it specific? Have you specified exactly what argument you are making? A strong argument will not only make a claim, but will also give some sense of how that claim is going to be made by mentioning specific terms or ideas that relate to the argument.

d. Does it answer the question "and so"? Does the argument just point to a connection, or does it go beyond that to make a claim about one of the essays based on the connection?

e. Does every paragraph relate to the argument? Each paragraph of your paper should somehow be proving your argument. Read each paragraph and ask yourself what it's doing. Ask how it helps to prove your argument.

f. Does the paper end with the same argument it started with? After you have written your draft, read your conclusion. Sometimes we're not sure what we want to write, but as we actually start writing we discover it along the way. Check your conclusion and see if you proved what you set out to prove. If not, it might be a good idea to use the ideas in your conclusion to revise your introduction and argument.

Arg-O-Meter

Use this peer review sheet to examine your classmate's argument:

Your Name: Name of Paper's Author:

Arg-O-Meter	
Weak	Strong
Vague, general, can't find it, expressed only in terms of one essay, just expresses comparison/ contrast or similarity/dissimilarity.	Specific, clear, easy to locate, expressed in terms of both essays, answers the question "and so?"

In this assignment, you are evaluating the strength of the author's argument. Remember that having a clear, specific argument is one of the crucial tasks for passing ENC 1101. With that in mind, answer the following questions like your grade depended on it, since whoever is reading your paper will do the same for you.

1. Find the sentence with the argument and copy it down here. If you can't find one sentence that has the argument, start by pointing that out and then write a sentence or two which explains what you think they are trying to argue:

2. Is the argument expressed in terms of both essays? Does it make it clear how the author is using one essay to make a specific point about the other? If not, then try and reword their argument to include both essays here:

3. Does the argument answer "and so"? What point is the author making? What is the new thing we are learning about one of the essays? Answer these questions by completing the following sentence: "Originally I thought _____ about the essay but this argument makes me realize _____ instead." Complete the sentence here:

Name _____

■ Exercise

"What a Thesis Is Not"

by Jessica Murray-Cooke

© copyright 2008. Used with permission.

A Thesis Is Not:

- A highly opinionated, attacking statement. While a thesis should express your attitude toward your subject, it should not be dogmatic or overstated; it should not alienate your reader.

> Ex.: In typical scholarship boy form, Rodriguez is a horrible writer because the only thing he does is reword Hoggart.
>
> Correction: Rodriguez tends to reword Hoggart's writing instead of creating his own; therefore, Rodriguez is still a scholarship boy.

Ex.:

_____

_____

_____

Correction:

_____

_____

_____

A Thesis Is Not:

- An announcement

> Ex.: My essay will discuss whether a student pub should exist on campus.
>
> Correction: Student pubs should not exist on campus because half the student population is under the legal drinking age.

Ex.:

_____

_____

_____

Correction:

_____

_____

_____

A Thesis Is Not:

- A factual statement—a thesis must be arguable. It must be centered around an issue that can be developed and can lead to further discussion and debate. Two facts that seem to stand in conflict are not a thesis either, but a thesis can be made of them.

> Ex.: In 1492 Columbus sailed the ocean blue.
>
> Correction: Most history textbooks report that Christopher Columbus discovered America in 1492, even though there were already millions of people living in the Americas when he arrived; this brings into question what is meant by the word "discover," and the accuracy of history textbooks.

Ex.:

_____

_____

_____

Correction:

_____

_____

_____

A Thesis Is Not:

• A broad statement or a vague and sweeping generalization.

> Ex.: Nowadays, high school education is meaningless.

Correction:

_____

_____

_____

Ex.:

_____

_____

_____

Correction:

_____

_____

_____

So, what *is* a thesis statement?

A thesis statement is a narrow, argumentative assertion about a topic which forms the backbone of an essay. The topic has to be questionable, meaning it can be argued. In other words, a thesis statement clearly states the writer's point of view but can still be argued by others. It opens up a debate, rather than shuts one down.

Name _____

■ Exercise
Argument and Evidence

1. Choose one paragraph from the essay you've been assigned to read.

    Separate each sentence out and analyze it individually.

    Mark it with an "A" if it is the author making an argument.

    Mark it with an "E" if it is the author offering evidence.

2. Choose one paragraph from a classmate's essay.

    Separate each sentence out and analyze it individually.

    Mark it with an "A" if it is the author making an argument.

    Mark it with an "E" if it is the author offering evidence.

    An essay must have both argument and evidence.

What are argument and evidence?
An **argument** is a debatable and persuasive statement. Debatable means people can and will disagree with it. Persuasive means that the author, knowing that it is debatable, does his best to convince others that they should agree, not disagree, with his point of view.

Evidence is very useful to an argument. It can be a quotation or a fact. It can be an anecdote or a statistic. It supports the argument and makes it more convincing or persuasive.

Examples:

My uncle returned from Iraq in 1991 with the symptoms of PTSD.

This is evidence. The author is probably using her uncle's experience as an example to support a point she is making.

He goes on to say that economic competition can stand in for warfare.

This is evidence. While the idea that economic competition can stand in for warfare is clearly an argument, here the idea is being paraphrased by another writer ("he says") and used as evidence to support her thesis.

We need a president with strong military instincts.

This is an argument. The author might follow this statement up with evidence from history, or hypothetical examples that would show situations in which the president will benefit from having strong military instincts.

His ideas, if pursued, would lead to widespread hunger and civil collapse.

This is an argument. The author probably prefaced this argument with an explanation of the ideas in question, and will follow this statement up with evidence from history, hypothetical examples, and logical reasoning which shows that the expected result of those ideas are hunger and civil collapse.

Section 3

EVIDENCE/QUOTATION/SUPPORT

Approaches to Using Quotation

Central to writing a successful paper in this class is the ability to work closely with quotations from the texts. In all of the papers you write for this course you will be making an argument, which we might call your thesis or project. In order to prove that argument, you will need to support it with evidence from the texts, and that evidence comes in the form of quotation.

There's a big difference between *having* quotations in a paper and *using* quotations. If you simply include quotations at different points in your own text, then your paper has quotation. But you need to provide some analysis of the quotations, analysis that guides the reader through an interpretation that supports your argument—that's *using* the quotation.

Learning how to use quotation isn't easy. It's one of the skills you will work on throughout the semester and, in fact, one of the skills you will continue to develop through the rest of your academic career. The activities in this section will give you a start on that process by providing you with practice on how to use quotation, both how to incorporate the text of others in your own text and how to apply those quotations to the larger project of your paper.

Introduction to Quotation

Why Quote?

We've all found ourselves in bad conversations. You pour your heart out only to discover that your friend is half-listening, if listening at all. When she responds, she has little to say: "Uh huh, okay, whatever," she says. Or when she responds, she changes the subject, proving that the whole time you were talking she was ignoring you, just waiting for her turn to speak. "Ha ha, yeah, that's nice. So anyway..."

Essays written in response to essays are a great deal like a conversation. Whether that conversation is a good one or a bad one is up to you. Are you going to be the one who has nothing to add? The one who just changes the subject and goes off on his own tangent? Or are you going to engage the essay writer in meaningful conversation? A good way to make a good conversation happen is through *quotes*.

In any *good* conversation, you refer to things other people have said:

> MIKE: Just like Annie said when she got back from her first skydiving trip, "you don't know what it's like until you do it." And I agree with her. Anyone who has never been skydiving can't claim not to like it. You won't know until you try!

When Mike refers to Annie's words, his arguments benefit from the fact that Annie is more of an authority on skydiving than he is, because she's done it. Notice that he doesn't just repeat her words; he introduces her words ("Just like Annie said when she got back") to make clear who said them, and when she said them, to give them context. He also comments on what she has said (he agrees with her!), and he adds something ("Anyone who has never been," Mike says, "can't claim not to like [skydiving]." He believes that "you won't know" if you like it "until you try!").

You may agree or disagree with the words you quote, ask a question based upon them, or take the ideas a step further—but you must add something:

BRIT: I don't think that's what Annie meant. I don't have to jump out of an airplane to know that I'd hate it. I don't like speed, heights, or airplanes! Annie also said she "always wanted to do it," and that she "always imagined it would be great, but it was even better." She meant that her imagination wasn't as intense as the real thing; Annie always knew that she would like skydiving, long before she ever did it.

Just like a good contribution to a conversation, a good essay requires engaging with the ideas of others; that means that sometimes you will describe, paraphrase, or quote someone else's points, then respond to them. When you do this, you need to give credit where credit is due. If you quote or refer to specific information, you must cite: citing is a skill that you will use frequently.

Bonus Question: Who is better representing Annie's views, Mike or Brit? How can you tell?

_____

_____

_____

_____

_____

Name _____

■ Exercise

Responding to Quotation

You've read the assigned essay, and you've underlined passages that struck you as particularly interesting, important, original, etc.

In this exercise, you will begin responding to those passages. It may help to think of this process as you having a "conversation" with the author of the essay: he/she is saying things that are interesting or important, and you (by underlining) are replying, "hey, that's interesting!" or "hey, that's important!" Now imagine the next step: the author replies, "why do you find that interesting or important?" Answering that question is the goal of this exercise.

1. Select the most interesting/important quotation from the essay, and copy it here:

   _____
   _____
   _____

2. Explain **why** you find this passage particularly interesting/important:

   _____
   _____
   _____

3. Building on what's interesting/important about this passage, take the idea even further:

   _____
   _____
   _____

Repeat this process with at least three additional quotations from the essay:

1. Select another interesting/important quotation from the essay, and copy it here:

   _____
   _____
   _____

2. Explain **why** you find this passage particularly interesting/important:

   _____
   _____
   _____

3. Building on what's interesting/important about this passage, take the idea even further:

    _____

    _____

    _____

1. Select a third interesting/important quotation from the essay, and copy it here:

    _____

    _____

    _____

2. Explain **why** you find this passage particularly interesting/important:

    _____

    _____

    _____

3. Building on what's interesting/important about this passage, take the idea even further:

    _____

    _____

    _____

1. Select a fourth interesting/important quotation from the essay, and copy it here:

    _____

    _____

    _____

2. Explain **why** you find this passage particularly interesting/important:

    _____

    _____

    _____

3. Building on what's interesting/important about this passage, take the idea even further:

_____

_____

_____

1. Select a fifth interesting/important quotation from the essay, and copy it here:

_____

_____

_____

2. Explain **why** you find this passage particularly interesting/important:

_____

_____

_____

3. Building on what's interesting/important about this passage, take the idea even further:

_____

_____

_____

Name _____

■ Exercise

Connection

Connecting Two Essays

Your assignment may require you to "find connections" between two different essays. This exercise will help you bring the ideas of two essays together into a single essay of your own.

Part One: Nail That Connection!

1. Select two quotations you think make a connection, one from each essay.

    Q1: _____

    _____

    _____

    _____

    Q2: _____

    _____

    _____

    _____

2. **Circle** the phrases in each quotation that you think actually connect and **draw a line** connecting them.

3. Write a sentence in which you explain the connection **using each of those phrases**.

    Connection: _____

    _____

    _____

4. Expand on this sentence to create your analysis of these quotations. Be sure to **explain how** these quotations support your argument/thesis.

    Analysis: _____

    _____

    _____

Repeat for the next connection. Not only do you get to see the pieces of text next to each other, which helps you see the connection between them, but you also refer directly to the quotations as you explain the connection, and to the exact pieces of the quotation that actually connect. If you can't find phrases that connect in each quotation, then perhaps you should choose different passages.

Connection #2:

Q1: _____

_____

_____

_____

Q2: _____

_____

_____

_____

Connection: _____

_____

_____

Analysis: _____

_____

_____

Connection #3:

Q1: _____

_____

_____

_____

Q2: _____

_____

_____

_____

Connection: _____

_____

_____

Analysis: _____

_____

Name _____

Part Two: Barclay's Super-Secret Formula for Connection

$$C_1 \equiv I \rightarrow Q_1 \rightarrow E \rightarrow T \rightarrow Q_2 \rightarrow C_e$$

C_1 = Start by stating your claim, what you are trying to prove.

I = Then introduce the first quotation.

Q_1 = Give the first quotation.

E = Explain it in your own words.

T = Give some sort of transition to the next quotation, providing a clue to connection.

Q_2 = Give the second quote.

C_e = Explain how the second quote connects to the first one in a sentence or two. This last part is crucial. You need to explain the connection in order to really prove it.

Connection #1:

C_1 _____

_____

I _____

_____

Q_1 _____

_____

E _____

_____

T _____

_____

Q_2 _____

_____

C_e _____

_____

Connection #2:

C_1 _____

_____

I _____

_____

Q_1 _____

_____

E _____

_____

T _____

_____

Q_2 _____

_____

C_e _____

_____

Connection #3:

C_1 _____

_____

I _____

_____

Q_1 _____

_____

E _____

_____

T _____

_____

Name _____

Q_2 _____

_____

C_e _____

_____

Part Three: Conn-X-ionator

The conn-X-ionator is a peer-review exercise that will help you and your classmates sharpen and strengthen the connections in your essays.

Your Name: Name of Paper's Author:

Conn-X-ionator	
Weak	Strong
Assumed, not explained; brief mention without clear explanation; doesn't "follow through"; doesn't relate to argument; doesn't use quotes from both texts.	Uses the super-secret formula; clearly relates to the argument; does a good job of explaining just how the two quotes connect and how that connection relates to the argument.

In this assignment, you are evaluating the strength of the author's connections. Remember that having a clear, specific argument is one of the crucial tasks for passing ENC 1101. With that in mind, answer the following questions like your grade depended on it, since whoever is reading your paper will do the same for you.

1. Choose a body paragraph at random. Does it have a connection? Put a big star in the paper next to the paragraph you've chosen. In the margin, put Q_1 next to the first quote, Q_2 next to the second quote, and C_e next to the explanation of the connection. Does this paragraph have all three elements? If it does, then explain why the connection is good here. If it does not, tell the author how to make this connection stronger here:

2. Check each body paragraph for connection. If you find one without a connection, put a giant exclamation point in the margins. If you found a paragraph without connection, explain what that paragraph is doing in the paper here:

3. Are there any "floating quotes"? These are quotes that are not introduced and are not related to the surrounding text: they just kind of pop into the paper suddenly. If you find a floating quote, put a giant Fl in the margins and then explain here what needs to be done with the quote to make it work into the text:

4. Do the connections answer the question "and so"? Does the author simply say one essay is similar to (or different from) the other? If so, write down something that you learned about one of the essays from the connection even though the author doesn't point it out: (For example: "When you connected Kimmelman and Percy by saying _____, I realized that though _____ says _____, _____'s idea changes that because _____.)

5. If this paper is not yet long enough, you can help by suggesting other connections that would work with their argument. In the space below, give the author some direction on where to find more connections by pointing them to any incidents or examples or passages you remember from either of the essays:

Quotation: The Rules

The person reading your words should be able to distinguish, clearly, between your ideas and the ideas of others.

The reader should be able to locate the sources that you used and find the quotations that you chose very easily.

However, a good quotation should not necessarily send the reader running to the source to double-check it. A good citation should be:

Accurate: the words should be reproduced faithfully, and should accurately portray the author's intent.

Introduced: the reader should be told who has said this, and where.

Contextualized: the reader should have an idea of why this was said, and what the author's larger arguments are.

Honesty is a priority when quoting: represent the author's words in a way that is true to the author's intent. For example, if the author quotes or paraphrases another author, if the author describes a hypothetical argument with which he or she disagrees, do not pretend that these are the author's words.

Use single quotes within double quotes to indicate a quote within a quote.

Example

In "Arts of the Contact Zone," Mary Louise Pratt explains how an otherwise unknown Peruvian wrote a letter to the King of Spain in the form of the Spaniards' own histories, and how, by "writing a 'new chronicle,' Guaman Poma took over the official Spanish genre for his own ends" (Pratt 519).

There Is More Than One Kind of Citation

The object of citation is to make the source information easily accessible to the reader. There is obviously more than one way that this could be done. Certain areas of study put a higher priority on one type of information over another: in English, page numbers are important. In sociology, the year in which a study was performed or a paper issued is more important. That's why you'll see names and page numbers in parentheses in the middle of English papers, and names and years in the middle of sociology papers. Different disciplines use different rules for citation. Depending upon the variety of courses you take in your college career, you may become acquainted with many of them. Remember that citation is important: it may seem like a tedious detail, but it is not. Putting your information into proper form is necessary to communicate your engagement with sources, and is a vital skill.

Name _____

■ Exercise

Introducing, Quoting, Punctuating, Citing, Commenting

Choose a quote about which you have an opinion. Introduce that quote—e.g., *In "Haunted America," Patricia Nelson Limerick marvels that the Modoc War*—give the quote—*"turned colorful, quaint, and marketable in an amazingly short time"*—make sure to punctuate correctly while citing—*(Limerick 434).*—and comment on the quote—*This is a classic example of how civilizations rewrite history to please their tastes. Once it was won, the Modoc War went from a bloody, chaotic series of mistakes to a marketable commodity, entertainment for the kids.*

Now it's your turn! Remember: introduce, quote, punctuate, cite, and comment.

_____

_____

_____

_____

_____

_____

_____

_____

Do it again: introduce, quote, punctuate, cite, and comment.

_____

_____

_____

_____

_____

_____

_____

_____

Name _____

■ Exercise
Integrating Quotation into Your Sentences

Part One

1. **Choose** an interesting and/or important quotation from the essay you're reading.

2. **Introduce** and **present** the quotation:

    _____

    _____

    _____

3. Add **context** and **give commentary** (agreement, disagreement) on the quotation:

    _____

    _____

    _____

4. Now, **integrate** the quotation into your introduction, contexualization, and commentary, so that everything appears in just one grammatically-correct sentence:

    _____

    _____

    _____

5. Rewrite the integrated sentence so it is clear and direct, and no longer than necessary:

    _____

    _____

    _____

6. Rewrite once more if necessary.

    _____

    _____

    _____

7. Add a citation to the finished sentence, and make sure the punctuation is correct.

    _____

    _____

    _____

Part Two

Using the final sentence from part one as a model, compose two more integrated quotation sentences:

1. (Introduce, quote, contextualize, comment, cite, punctuate):

    _____

    _____

    _____

2. (Introduce, quote, contextualize, comment, cite, punctuate):

    _____

    _____

    _____

ORGANIZATION

Paragraphs

Paragraphs are mostly a *visual* convenience: readers have trouble focusing on long, endless-seeming blocks of text. We prefer our text in bite-size portions. And we prefer those portions to be ordered, not random.

For these reasons, paragraphs must try to organize themselves around a central idea; when a new idea presents itself, it is time for a new paragraph. If an idea is complex and requires, say, 16–20 sentences to be explained, we prefer to break down those sentences into two or three portions, determined by shifts among minor ideas within the larger idea. These are not "rules," but general guidelines that will make your writing better organized and easier to read.

You will see these guidelines flouted and outright ignored in some of the essays that you read for this class: you will see "paragraphs" of only one or two sentences; you will see very long blocks of text far exceeding 20 sentences. That is because these are (again) not "rules" but guidelines, and very talented writers like to push the limits of what is possible, and show their skill in manipulating rhythm and tone with variants of the generally accepted guidelines for writing. This is part of an author's style. You too are developing your own style, but at the student level (in fact, at the level of most writers, students or not!), it is a good idea to stick close to the guidelines, unless you have a compelling reason for doing otherwise.

Creating paragraphs is more art than science, but as a general rule, a double-spaced 8 ½ × 11 inch page of essay should be broken down into two or three paragraphs. A paragraph should generally fall between four and seven sentences and should focus on one main idea. A sentence that sums up the main idea of a paragraph is called a "topic sentence."

In the case of an academic essay written in response to another essay (which is what you are writing), each paragraph should be expected to contain some support (evidence, examples, facts, quotations) for your argument. Each paragraph should also be expected to contain some of the argument itself. All paragraphs except for the last one should transition nicely into the paragraph that follows it. Finally, the concluding paragraph should give your essay a feeling of resolution, completion, and finality.

Essay and Paragraph Structure

This drawing represents one concept for a strongly structured essay:

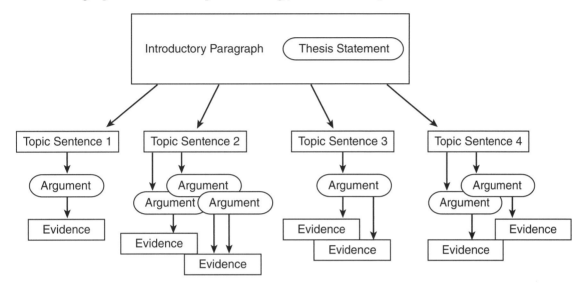

Each down-flowing grouping containing a topic sentence and some combination of arguments and evidence is a paragraph.

Notice the overall structure: an abundance of evidence is used to support arguments, which then support topic sentences, which all support the thesis statement, which is given in the introductory paragraph.

Keep in mind that in this example there are four supportive paragraphs, but there could just as well be three or five or six or more, depending on the length and depth the essay will achieve.

Also keep in mind that depending upon the paragraph and the arguments being made, there may be one or two (or even three) arguments in support of the topic sentence. Notice that every argument needs support from evidence.

You'll see in this example that in some cases two related arguments may be supported by one piece of evidence, and that, likewise, one argument may be supported by two pieces of evidence. It all depends on what is most appropriate to the situation.

Lastly, notice that this drawing doesn't take the concluding paragraph into account—that is one more paragraph that, like the introduction, plays by a different set of rules, and we'll address the introduction and conclusion separately.

Name _____

■ Exercise

Charting Your Paragraphs

For this exercise, you will draw a chart of each of your paragraphs, similar to the example on page 77, except that instead of writing the word "argument" you will copy down the argument you're making; instead of writing "evidence" you'll copy down the evidence used, and where it says "thesis statement" and "topic sentence," you will copy down your thesis statement and topic sentences in full.

1. Chart your first body paragraph	2. Chart your second body paragraph

Analyze the Charts

Are your paragraphs lacking a true topic sentence, one that makes clear the purpose of the paragraph? If so, decide on the purpose of the paragraph now, and add it in.

Are your paragraphs lacking evidence? Do they simply talk and talk without giving examples? If so, find examples that fit the paragraph now, and add them.

Are your paragraphs lacking argument? Do they simply give evidence and more evidence (are they summary?) without explaining what any of it has to do with the topic or thesis, or what the point is? If so, you might need to cut some of the evidence given, and explain what the evidence that you don't remove *proves*.

For this exercise, you will draw a chart of each of your paragraphs, similar to the example on page 77, except that instead of writing the word "argument" you will copy down the argument you're making; instead of writing "evidence" you'll copy down the evidence used, and where it says "thesis statement" and "topic sentence," you will copy down your thesis statement and topic sentences in full.

3. Chart your third body paragraph	4. Chart your fourth body paragraph

Analyze the Charts

Are your paragraphs lacking a true topic sentence, one that makes clear the purpose of the paragraph? If so, decide on the purpose of the paragraph now, and add it in.

Are your paragraphs lacking evidence? Do they simply talk and talk without giving examples? If so, find examples that fit the paragraph now, and add them.

Are your paragaphs lacking argument? Do they simply give evidence and more evidence (are they summary?) without explaining what any of it has to do with the topic or thesis, or what the point is? If so, you might need to cut some of the evidence given, and explain what the evidence that you don't remove *proves*.

Name _____

■ Exercise

Paragraphing

For this exercise, you will take three paragraphs that you have drafted, and you will change them to fit the formulas provided for you.

1. Choose a paragraph which gives an excellent, illustrative example. Now, rearrange its sentences so that they appear in this order:

   a. The example is given in 2–3 sentences. (evidence)

   b. The connection between the example and the thesis is given in 1 sentence. (argument)

   c. This connection's relevance to the thesis statement is explained in 1 sentence. (argument)

   d. Sum up the paragraph. (topic sentence)

   e. Introduce the next paragraph. (transition)

a. _____

_____

b. _____

_____

_____

c. _____

_____

d. _____

_____

e. _____

_____

2. Choose a paragraph which makes a logical argument (this may be an argument structured, "if this, then that," or an argument that explains a cause-and-effect relationship). Now, rearrange the sentences so they appear in the following order:

    a. Explain in 1 sentence what will be shown or proven in this paragraph. (topic sentence)

    b. Make a logical argument in 2–3 sentences ("cause-effect," "if this, that," etc.). (argument)

    c. Introduce and give a quotation that provides support for your argument. (evidence)

    d. Explain how the quotation has proven your point in 1 sentence. (argument)

    e. Introduce the next paragraph. (transition)

a. _____

_____

b. _____

_____

_____

c. _____

_____

d. _____

_____

e. _____

_____

3. Choose a paragraph which primarily explains a quotation. Now, rearrange the sentences so they appear in the following order:

   a. Explain in 1 sentence what will be shown or proven in this paragraph. (topic sentence)

   b. Introduce and give a quotation that provides support for your argument. (evidence)

   c. Make a logical argument in 2–3 sentences. (argument)

   d. Explain how the quotation has proven your point in 1 sentence. (argument)

   e. Introduce the next paragraph. (transition)

a. _____

_____

b. _____

_____

_____

c. _____

_____

d. _____

_____

e. _____

_____

BONUS EXERCISE: Choose a paragraph that you feel is exceptionally strong from your own essay, a classmate's essay, or from an appropriately sized paragraph from the readings. Analyze the paragraph's use of a topic sentence, argument, evidence, and transition.

a. Does the paragraph contain a sentence that sums up its purpose?

    _____

    _____

b. What, in the paragraph, is evidence given to prove a point?

    _____

    _____

    _____

c. What, in the paragraph, is argumentative or persuasive speech?

    _____

    _____

    _____

d. How does the paragraph transition?

    _____

    _____

Name _____

■ Exercise

Transitions

Transitions Link the Pieces of Your Paper Together

Transitions are a matter both of logic and style: they show connections between your ideas, and they also make your paper flow smoothly for the reader.

You may need a transition between major parts of your argument, or you may need transitions between paragraphs. You may even need transitions within a single paragraph. If you are moving from one idea to another you need a transition.

Part One

List Transition Words/Phrases

As a group, develop your list of transition words and phrases. Start by brainstorming, and then extend your list by examining the transitions used in the essays you've read so far. Then examine the essays you've written for class for transitions you've been using.

Transition Word

conversely _____   _____   _____   _____

_____   _____   _____   _____

_____   _____   _____   _____

_____   _____   _____   _____

_____   _____   _____   _____

_____   _____   _____   _____

_____   _____   _____   _____

_____   _____   _____   _____

_____   _____   _____   _____

_____   _____   _____   _____

Note that there are different types of transition: the example given to start you off, "conversely," is a transition to contrast, but "likewise" is also a transition word. It introduces something that is similar.

Go down the list of transition words and determine what each is doing. Is it making a comparison? Drawing a distinction? Giving an additional example in support of the same point? Segueing into a detailed description? Providing a definition? Introducing an example? What else can you discover transitions doing?

Part Two

Compose Transition Sentences

Find three places in your paper that desperately need a transition. Fix them by building a new sentence that uses one or more of the transitions from your list. Write your new sentences below:

1. _____

_____

_____

_____

_____

2. _____

_____

_____

_____

_____

3. _____

_____

_____

_____

_____

Name _____

■ Exercise

Introductions
by Janelle Garcia

Your introduction is the first impression a reader gets from your essay, so it should be a good one. You want to provide the necessary information, but not too much information.

A strong introduction will serve as a guiding force for you throughout your essay, indicating when you have moved off topic and which ideas you should explore next.

But perhaps the most useful function of your introduction is as a set of directions. The best directions give you enough details so that you know which turns to take and which landmarks to expect. Bad directions can be too vague, or they might contain unnecessary details and explanations. Either way, they lose you. Make sure your introduction is specific to your essay, so readers can expect where the essay will take them and how many twists and turns are on the way.

Introduction Functions:

- Pique the reader's interest: Your introduction should hook the reader.

- Introduce the authors and readings you plan to incorporate into your essay and explain their relevance.

- State your overall argument. Generally, your thesis statement should be placed in the introduction.

- Outline the main ideas you'll explore, in the order you will discuss them.

Part One

Introduction Snapshot

1. Start with the introduction of the published, professional essay you are reading. (Depending on the writer's style, it might be broken into more than one paragraph, but look at function over indentation or spacing.) Based only on the introduction, sketch an outline of the main points and ideas you expect the essay to explore.

2. Discussion: do the readings have traditional introductory paragraphs? Would a clearer introduction help you, as a reader, navigate through the reading? Is the introduction successful? Is there anything about the introduction you would change?

3. Rewrite the author's introduction to make it clearer and more useful to the reader.

    _____

    _____

    _____

    _____

    _____

    _____

    _____

    _____

    How would changing the introduction impact the remainder of the reading?

    _____

    _____

4. Now exchange essays with a classmate. Based only on your classmate's introduction, sketch a rough outline of the main points and ideas you expect the remaining essay to explore. Share your expectations with the writer.

Additional Questions

5. Based on your introduction, did your reader expect anything from your essay that you weren't planning to write about?

    _____

    _____

6. Based on your introduction, did your reader not get some of the things that you were planning to write about?

    _____

    _____

7. Is it possible to know exactly what the essay will discuss based on the introduction?

    _____

8. Did you find yourself wanting the details of the essay to follow the order suggested by the introduction?

    _____

    _____

Name _____

■ Exercise

After Outlines

Outlines are useful to write before you start composing your essay because they let you know where you're going. They provide a good structural backbone for your paper, and they keep you on track. Outlines don't have to be elaborate with Roman numerals and letters and numbers and more letters and more numbers. An outline can be as simple as "State the problem, Show the problem, Solve the problem."

Outlines can also be useful after you've written a draft. They show you how you've put your paper together, and give you a quick roadmap to weak paragraphs and things that need improvement. Try this post-draft outline to track the flow of your argument:

1. Start by writing a one-sentence summary of every paragraph in your paper. If you find a paragraph that you can't summarize in one sentence, examine it closely. Do you have more than one idea in that paragraph? Should you break it into two? Or are you simply not expressing yourself clearly? How can you fix it?

2. Examine each paragraph for two things: 1) evidence, support—quotes and facts that support your argument—and 2) persuasive argument, connection. Every paragraph should have some evidence and some argument connection. If you have paragraphs with only connection or only evidence, this outline will help you to spot them, so that you can fix them.

Your instructor may ask you to type and submit your after outline as a draft or as part of your assignment.

Outline

I. Thesis: [Your thesis statement goes here]: _____

_____

_____

II. P2: [Paragraph Two's topic sentence goes here]: _____

_____

   A. Argument

      1. [A logical/persuasive sentence that supports this paragraph's topic sentence]:

_____

      2. [Another logical/persuasive sentence that supports this paragraph's topic sentence]:

_____

B. Evidence

    1. [A fact or quote that you cite which supports or "proves" one of your argumentative sentences; cite]: _____ ( )

    2. [Another fact or quote which supports or "proves" one of your argumentative sentences; cite]:

    _____ ( )

III. P3: Topic Sentence: _____

    A. Argument

        1. _____

        2. _____

        3. _____

    B. Evidence

        1. _____

        2. _____

IV. P4: Topic Sentence: _____

    A. Argument

        1. _____

        2. _____

    B. Evidence

        1. _____

        2. _____

        3. _____

    …et cetera

After Outline
Notes:
- The number of paragraphs in an essay varies.

- The number of arguments and pieces of evidence given in a paragraph varies, and are not always equal (one point may be supported by 2 or more pieces of evidence; 2 or more arguments may be supported by one piece of evidence, etc.).

- Your typed outline will be double-spaced, and will have your name, your instructor's name, the date, and the assignment written in the top left corner.

- You put your last name in the top right corner using your word processor's HEADER function.

- If you submit your outline with your essay, you will begin numbering the first page of your essay where your outline leaves off: if your outline is 3 pages, your essay begins on page 4.

Using the outline:
- Make sure your thesis is clear and sums up your objectives in this essay.

- Make sure your topic sentences organize the subtopics of your thesis.

- Make sure each argument is in the appropriate paragraph (as defined by the topic sentences).

- Make sure your arguments support your thesis (and that they do not go off-topic).

- Make sure that all of your arguments are accompanied by supporting evidence.

- Make sure that the evidence you cite in a given paragraph supports the argument being made *in that paragraph*.

3. You now have the topic sentence, support, and connection of each paragraph. Go over them, checking the flow of your argument. Do the sentences seem to follow logically? Does your argument flow? Are there sections that seem out of place or off-track? Are there two or three paragraphs in a row with no support? Is something missing? How can you fix it?

4. Now check for the organization of your paper. Is there any section that seems out of place? Where does it belong: later in your paper? Earlier? Does it not belong at all? Have you broken a section into too many or too few pieces? How can you fix it?

5. Finally, use this outline to plan your next revision. Where in your current draft do you need to revise? Where will you expand and include new material?

REVISION

Three Types of Revision

Global Revision

- Writing does not respond to the task.

- Ideas are underdeveloped and/or weak and/or biased.

- Organization is unclear and/or ineffective.

- Argument logic is unsound and/or untraceable.

- Content is superficial and/or contains factual errors.

- Writing style, format, and presentation are incomplete.

- Requires corrections.

- Major overhaul of the paper.

- Requires 70–100% rewrite.

- Sections and paragraphs rewritten, rearranged, added, and/or scrapped.

- Retained sections and paragraphs elaborated, qualified, and/or extended.

Conceptual Revision

- Writing responds to the task unsuccessfully and/or incompletely.

- Ideas show signs of incomplete development.

- Organization is ineffective and/or unobvious.

- Argument logic is weak and/or biased and/or unrefined.

- Content is casual and/or clumsy.

- Writing style, format, and presentation are unpolished.

- Requires corrections.

- Ideas worth keeping and rethinking.

- Prose needs rewriting.

- Requires 45–70% rewrite.

- Crafts a new response to the prompt with the same ideas.

- Sections and paragraphs rewritten, rearranged, added, and/or scrapped.

- Ideas and/or positions get rethought, revisited, extended, and elaborated.

Local Revision

- Writing responds to the task productively although perhaps not comprehensively.

- Ideas are developed reasonably well although perhaps not completely.

- Organization is clear although may not consistently support ideas and/or thesis.

- Argument logic is sound although could be bolstered with additional support.

- Content is serious and thoughtful.

- Writing style, format, and presentation are skillful and appropriate although would be improved with meticulous revisions.

- Requires corrections.

- Requires 25–45% rewrite.

- Sentence-level tinkering for precise and elegant expression.

- Word search for most effective diction and turn of phrase.

- Transitional focus to enhance connections between sentences and paragraphs.

- Sections and paragraphs rewritten, rearranged, added, and/or scrapped.

We would like to thank and acknowledge Dr. David Bartholomae and Dr. Jeffrey Galin for providing the conceptual foundation of this document.

Reviewer's Name _____

■ Exercise
Peer Review #1: Simple Review

Paper Author: _____

Paper Title: _____

1. Place an asterisk next to the one sentence that contains the argument. Then paraphrase the argument in this space. How specific is it? Does it address the assignment? Do you see any problems it might cause? Could someone argue with it? Don't answer all these questions, but after paraphrasing the argument, discuss it briefly:

2. Place a check mark next to places where you see connection and quotation being used very well. What makes these instances effective? Do they connect essays directly? Do they support the argument? Briefly discuss the author's use of quotation:

3. Briefly discuss the way in which the author connects the essays. Does it feel sufficient and balanced?

Reviewer's Name _____

■ Exercise

Peer Review #1: Simple Review

Paper Author: _____

Paper Title: _____

1. Place an asterisk next to the one sentence that contains the argument. Then paraphrase the argument in this space. How specific is it? Does it address the assignment? Do you see any problems it might cause? Could someone argue with it? Don't answer all these questions, but after paraphrasing the argument, discuss it briefly:

2. Place a check mark next to places where you see connection and quotation being used very well. What makes these instances effective? Do they connect essays directly? Do they support the argument? Briefly discuss the author's use of quotation:

3. Briefly discuss the way in which the author connects the essays. Does it feel sufficient and balanced?

Reviewer's Name _____

■ Exercise

Peer Review #1: Simple Review

Paper Author: _____

Paper Title: _____

1. Place an asterisk next to the one sentence that contains the argument. Then paraphrase the argument in this space. How specific is it? Does it address the assignment? Do you see any problems it might cause? Could someone argue with it? Don't answer all these questions, but after paraphrasing the argument, discuss it briefly:

2. Place a check mark next to places where you see connection and quotation being used very well. What makes these instances effective? Do they connect essays directly? Do they support the argument? Briefly discuss the author's use of quotation:

3. Briefly discuss the way in which the author connects the essays. Does it feel sufficient and balanced?

Section 6

Reviewer's Name _____

■ Exercise

Peer Review #2: Computer Classroom

Open up a word processor and create a new document. Begin by typing:

REVIEWER: Your name

AUTHOR: Name of person who wrote the paper you're reviewing

ESSAY TITLE: The title of the essay you're reviewing

Begin by reading through the paper and completing a normal peer revision, paying particular attention to things like the argument and the use of quotation. Make thoughtful comments in the margins (Insert → Comment, or use the Markup Toolbar). Write summary end comments as well.

When you're done with the first read-through, type responses to the following questions in the word processor and then print out two copies, one for the author and one for your instructor:

- **Evaluate the Argument**. Place a star on the paper next to the argument and then type up a paragraph that summarizes and evaluates this argument. You should start the paragraph with a one-sentence summary of the argument "The author argues that . . ." Then evaluate the strengths and weaknesses of the argument in the rest of the paragraph.

- **Evaluate the Use of Text**. Look at each quotation used in the paper and mark in the margin: "1" if it summarizes, defines, restates; "2" if it works with another quotation to make a connection between the texts (mark the other quotation "2" as well); "3" if the author stops to analyze the quotation in terms of her or his argument. When completed, look over the use of quotation. Then compose a paragraph analyzing the author's quotation usage: is there a predominance of a certain type? Is there a particularly good use of quotation? Where? Is there a place where quotation is needed, or the kind of use of quotation should be changed? Where?

- **Evaluate Organization**. In the word processor, type a one-sentence summary of every paragraph in the body of the paper. Then briefly evaluate the effectiveness of the organization: do the paragraphs proceed in a logical order? Should something be re-arranged? Is each paragraph focused on a single point, and does that point participate in the larger project?

- **Addressing the Essays**. Are there any areas where the author seems to be overlooking a piece of one or the other texts in the interest of making things fit his or her argument? Are there sections the author needs to consider in one of the essays? Briefly point out to the author where she or he should look to insure textual responsibility.

Return the paper to its author with a printed copy of your evaluative responses. Give your instructor a copy of these responses as well. If you do not complete this by the end of class, work on it at home and bring it for the instructor and the paper's author for the next class.

Reviewer's Name _____

■ Exercise

Peer Review #3: Group Questions

1. Identify the argument. Where is it being made? What does the paper's author want to say, and does she or he say it clearly? Paraphrase from your memory of what the writer said, and then return to the essay to see if your version matches up.

2. What are the major terms of the essay? Are they defined clearly? How are they defined?

3. Where does the writer quote text? How does she or he use the quotes? Do they fit in with the rest of what the writer is saying? Are they explained (discussed directly) before and/or after they appear?

4. Pick one paragraph where using text directly could have added to the strength of what the writer is saying, and discuss it in your comments.

5. Look at a paragraph that's just summary of the text without evidence that the writer is saying anything about it. Show how it might be different.

6. Look at the opening paragraph(s). Can you suggest ways that the point could be made more clearly? Concisely? Effectively?

7. Does the writer's style seem appropriate to her or his topic? Does it influence the content? How?

8. How are transitions made in the essay from point to point? Are they effective? In making transitions, is there ever a wrenching quality or an unnaturalness to the flow of logic or sequence?

9. Did the writer "do" the assignment, as you understand it? How so? How not?

10. Identify specific places where you were confused by the language, the movement, or the argument of the paper, and talk about them in comments.

11. Identify specific places where the essay engaged you most as a reader (either where it was most interesting or most upsetting) and talk about them in comments.

12. Does the writer conclude the essay with a different idea than she or he started with? Why might this shift in argument have happened? Or does the writer simply restate the original argument without having deepened or explored it to your satisfaction? How might a revision develop the main idea or argument further?

13. What does the writer want to teach you as a reader? Is it something you feel you already know? Is it something that surprises you, based on your prior experience of the writer? Does it change the way you read your own essay?

14. What is the one thing that this writer does well that you feel you also do well, or that you would like to work on in your own writing? Is her or his method of doing it the same as yours? Is there anything from her or his writing that you can "steal"?

Reviewer's Name _____

■ Exercise

Peer Review #3: Group Questions

1. Identify the argument. Where is it being made? What does the paper's author want to say, and does she or he say it clearly? Paraphrase from your memory of what the writer said, and then return to the essay to see if your version matches up.

2. What are the major terms of the essay? Are they defined clearly? How are they defined?

3. Where does the writer quote text? How does she or he use the quotes? Do they fit in with the rest of what the writer is saying? Are they explained (discussed directly) before and/or after they appear?

4. Pick one paragraph where using text directly could have added to the strength of what the writer is saying, and discuss it in your comments.

5. Look at a paragraph that's just summary of the text without evidence that the writer is saying anything about it. Show how it might be different.

6. Look at the opening paragraph(s). Can you suggest ways that the point could be made more clearly? Concisely? Effectively?

7. Does the writer's style seem appropriate to her or his topic? Does it influence the content? How?

8. How are transitions made in the essay from point to point? Are they effective? In making transitions, is there ever a wrenching quality or an unnaturalness to the flow of logic or sequence?

9. Did the writer "do" the assignment, as you understand it? How so? How not?

10. Identify specific places where you were confused by the language, the movement, or the argument of the paper, and talk about them in comments.

11. Identify specific places where the essay engaged you most as a reader (either where it was most interesting or most upsetting) and talk about them in comments.

12. Does the writer conclude the essay with a different idea than she or he started with? Why might this shift in argument have happened? Or does the writer simply restate the original argument without having deepened or explored it to your satisfaction? How might a revision develop the main idea or argument further?

13. What does the writer want to teach you as a reader? Is it something you feel you already know? Is it something that surprises you, based on your prior experience of the writer? Does it change the way you read your own essay?

14. What is the one thing that this writer does well that you feel you also do well, or that you would like to work on in your own writing? Is her or his method of doing it the same as yours? Is there anything from her or his writing that you can "steal"?

Reviewer's Name _____

■ Exercise

Peer Review #3: Group Questions

1. Identify the argument. Where is it being made? What does the paper's author want to say, and does she or he say it clearly? Paraphrase from your memory of what the writer said, and then return to the essay to see if your version matches up.

2. What are the major terms of the essay? Are they defined clearly? How are they defined?

3. Where does the writer quote text? How does she or he use the quotes? Do they fit in with the rest of what the writer is saying? Are they explained (discussed directly) before and/or after they appear?

4. Pick one paragraph where using text directly could have added to the strength of what the writer is saying, and discuss it in your comments.

5. Look at a paragraph that's just summary of the text without evidence that the writer is saying anything about it. Show how it might be different.

6. Look at the opening paragraph(s). Can you suggest ways that the point could be made more clearly? Concisely? Effectively?

7. Does the writer's style seem appropriate to her or his topic? Does it influence the content? How?

8. How are transitions made in the essay from point to point? Are they effective? In making transitions, is there ever a wrenching quality or an unnaturalness to the flow of logic or sequence?

9. Did the writer "do" the assignment, as you understand it? How so? How not?

10. Identify specific places where you were confused by the language, the movement, or the argument of the paper, and talk about them in comments.

11. Identify specific places where the essay engaged you most as a reader (either where it was most interesting or most upsetting) and talk about them in comments.

12. Does the writer conclude the essay with a different idea than she or he started with? Why might this shift in argument have happened? Or does the writer simply restate the original argument without having deepened or explored it to your satisfaction? How might a revision develop the main idea or argument further?

13. What does the writer want to teach you as a reader? Is it something you feel you already know? Is it something that surprises you, based on your prior experience of the writer? Does it change the way you read your own essay?

14. What is the one thing that this writer does well that you feel you also do well, or that you would like to work on in your own writing? Is her or his method of doing it the same as yours? Is there anything from her or his writing that you can "steal"?

■ Exercise

Peer Review #4: Simple Review 2

by Roseanne Marquart

Paper Author: _____

Read the draft through to get a sense of the writer's argument.

Introduction and Thesis Statement

- What specific reference does the writer use as background for the argument or discussion? (brief history related to topic, relevant anecdote, a quote, etc.)

- Are the title of the text and the author's full name mentioned in the Introductory paragraph?

- Is there a thesis or forecasting statement which indicates the writer's argument? *Underline it.*

Paragraphs

- Underline the topic (first) sentence of each paragraph.

- Does all the information in each paragraph relate to its topic sentence?

- Indicate the *specific subject* of every paragraph in the margins of every paragraph. *If there is more than one subject, mention both. (For instance, "color imagery" and "narrative point of view.")*

- Does each paragraph establish a point which is connected to the writer's thesis?

- Do any of the paragraphs seem out of place because they do not relate to the thesis statement? Which one/s? *Indicate in the margins.*

- Does each paragraph follow logically from the one before, providing a "next step" in the discussion? *If not, write, "Transition needed."*

Support

- Does the writer use textual support to demonstrate the points s/he is making?

- Do the quotes used confirm the *particular points* made?

- Are quotes introduced and explained in the writer's own words?

- Is all evidence properly cited in MLA style?

Conclusion

- Does the conclusion simply repeat the thesis, or does the conclusion attempt to synthesize, or draw together, the major points of the essay?

- How might the conclusion be improved?

Final Remarks

In a paragraph, evaluate the draft's potential. You want to say more than, "Great draft!" Or, "This draft needs a lot of work!" *Instead, indicate strong points as well as weaker ones and offer specific, constructive commentary.*

Reviewer's Name _____

■ Exercise

Peer Review #4: Simple Review 2

by Roseanne Marquart

Paper Author: _____

Read the draft through to get a sense of the writer's argument.

Introduction and Thesis Statement

- What specific reference does the writer use as background for the argument or discussion? (brief history related to topic, relevant anecdote, a quote, etc.)

- Are the title of the text and the author's full name mentioned in the Introductory paragraph?

- Is there a thesis or forecasting statement which indicates the writer's argument? *Underline it.*

Paragraphs

- Underline the topic (first) sentence of each paragraph.

- Does all the information in each paragraph relate to its topic sentence?

- Indicate the *specific subject* of every paragraph in the margins of every paragraph. *If there is more than one subject, mention both. (For instance, "color imagery" and "narrative point of view.")*

- Does each paragraph establish a point which is connected to the writer's thesis?

- Do any of the paragraphs seem out of place because they do not relate to the thesis statement? Which one/s? *Indicate in the margins.*

- Does each paragraph follow logically from the one before, providing a "next step" in the discussion? *If not, write, "Transition needed."*

Support

- Does the writer use textual support to demonstrate the points s/he is making?

- Do the quotes used confirm the *particular points* made?

- Are quotes introduced and explained in the writer's own words?

- Is all evidence properly cited in MLA style?

Conclusion

- Does the conclusion simply repeat the thesis, or does the conclusion attempt to synthesize, or draw together, the major points of the essay?

- How might the conclusion be improved?

Final Remarks

In a paragraph, evaluate the draft's potential. You want to say more than, "Great draft!" Or, "This draft needs a lot of work!" *Instead, indicate strong points as well as weaker ones and offer specific, constructive commentary.*

Reviewer's Name _____

■ Exercise

Peer Review #4: Simple Review 2

by Roseanne Marquart

Paper Author: _____

Read the draft through to get a sense of the writer's argument.

Introduction and Thesis Statement
- What specific reference does the writer use as background for the argument or discussion? (brief history related to topic, relevant anecdote, a quote, etc.)

- Are the title of the text and the author's full name mentioned in the Introductory paragraph?

- Is there a thesis or forecasting statement which indicates the writer's argument? *Underline it.*

Paragraphs
- Underline the topic (first) sentence of each paragraph.

- Does all the information in each paragraph relate to its topic sentence?

- Indicate the *specific subject* of every paragraph in the margins of every paragraph. *If there is more than one subject, mention both. (For instance, "color imagery" and "narrative point of view.")*

- Does each paragraph establish a point which is connected to the writer's thesis?

- Do any of the paragraphs seem out of place because they do not relate to the thesis statement? Which one/s? *Indicate in the margins.*

- Does each paragraph follow logically from the one before, providing a "next step" in the discussion? *If not, write, "Transition needed."*

Support
- Does the writer use textual support to demonstrate the points s/he is making?

- Do the quotes used confirm the *particular points* made?

- Are quotes introduced and explained in the writer's own words?

- Is all evidence properly cited in MLA style?

Conclusion
- Does the conclusion simply repeat the thesis, or does the conclusion attempt to synthesize, or draw together, the major points of the essay?

- How might the conclusion be improved?

Final Remarks
In a paragraph, evaluate the draft's potential. You want to say more than, "Great draft!" Or, "This draft needs a lot of work!" *Instead, indicate strong points as well as weaker ones and offer specific, constructive commentary.*

Reviewer's Name _____

■ Exercise

Peer Review #5: Grid and Assessment

by Jessica Murray-Cooke
Copyright 2008. Used with permission.

Opening Paragraph	Strongly Agree	Agree	Disagree	Strongly Disagree	Peer Comments and Revision Suggestions
Essay has a creative and original title.					
Opening sentence is original, unusual, or otherwise engaging.					
Provides a well-formulated and easily identifiable thesis statement.					
Closing Paragraph					
Offers a conclusive statement about the texts and task, rather than a simple summary of the texts and task.					
Ends on a skillful note, either employing a theme throughout the work or making a noteworthy closing comment.					
Sentence Level Issues					
Writer writes in a consistent medium to formal tone, avoids contractions and the use of the second person.					
Writer uses proper MLA citation practices for in-text quotations and provides an error sheet and Works Cited page.					
Writer creates effective transitions between sentences and paragraphs.					
Writer uses appropriate, informative, creative, and varied signal phrases.					

Task/Thesis Assessment Sheet
What Is the Task?
In the space provided, write what the assignment task is.

Strongest Paragraph
Tell the writer which paragraph you think is the strongest one, explaining specifically what makes it strong and accounting for how and where it responds effectively to the task and engages with the text(s).

Weakest Paragraph
Tell the writer which paragraph you think is the weakest one, explaining specifically what makes it weak and accounting for how and where it does not respond effectively to the task and/or disengages with the text(s).

What Is the Writer's Thesis?
Remember: a thesis statement is a narrow, argumentative assertion about a topic which forms the backbone of an essay. It alludes to evidence but does not necessarily "lay it all out" for the reader. The topic has to be questionable, meaning it can be argued. In other words, a thesis statement clearly states the writer's point of view but can still be argued by others. It opens up a debate, rather than shuts one down. Write below what you take to be the writer's thesis:

Reviewer's Name _____

■ Exercise

Peer Review #5: Grid and Assessment

by Jessica Murray-Cooke
Copyright 2008. Used with permission.

Opening Paragraph	Strongly Agree	Agree	Disagree	Strongly Disagree	Peer Comments and Revision Suggestions
Essay has a creative and original title.					
Opening sentence is original, unusual, or otherwise engaging.					
Provides a well-formulated and easily identifiable thesis statement.					
Closing Paragraph					
Offers a conclusive statement about the texts and task, rather than a simple summary of the texts and task.					
Ends on a skillful note, either employing a theme throughout the work or making a noteworthy closing comment.					
Sentence Level Issues					
Writer writes in a consistent medium to formal tone, avoids contractions and the use of the second person.					
Writer uses proper MLA citation practices for in-text quotations and provides an error sheet and Works Cited page.					
Writer creates effective transitions between sentences and paragraphs.					
Writer uses appropriate, informative, creative, and varied signal phrases.					

Task/Thesis Assessment Sheet
What Is the Task?
In the space provided, write what the assignment task is.

Strongest Paragraph
Tell the writer which paragraph you think is the strongest one, explaining specifically what makes it strong and accounting for how and where it responds effectively to the task and engages with the text(s).

Weakest Paragraph
Tell the writer which paragraph you think is the weakest one, explaining specifically what makes it weak and accounting for how and where it does not respond effectively to the task and/or disengages with the text(s).

What Is the Writer's Thesis?
Remember: a thesis statement is a narrow, argumentative assertion about a topic which forms the backbone of an essay. It alludes to evidence but does not necessarily "lay it all out" for the reader. The topic has to be questionable, meaning it can be argued. In other words, a thesis statement clearly states the writer's point of view but can still be argued by others. It opens up a debate, rather than shuts one down. Write below what you take to be the writer's thesis:

Reviewer's Name _____

■ Exercise

Peer Review #5: Grid and Assessment

by Jessica Murray-Cooke
Copyright 2008. Used with permission.

Opening Paragraph	Strongly Agree	Agree	Disagree	Strongly Disagree	Peer Comments and Revision Suggestions
Essay has a creative and original title.					
Opening sentence is original, unusual, or otherwise engaging.					
Provides a well-formulated and easily identifiable thesis statement.					
Closing Paragraph					
Offers a conclusive statement about the texts and task, rather than a simple summary of the texts and task.					
Ends on a skillful note, either employing a theme throughout the work or making a noteworthy closing comment.					
Sentence Level Issues					
Writer writes in a consistent medium to formal tone, avoids contractions and the use of the second person.					
Writer uses proper MLA citation practices for in-text quotations and provides an error sheet and Works Cited page.					
Writer creates effective transitions between sentences and paragraphs.					
Writer uses appropriate, informative, creative, and varied signal phrases.					

Task/Thesis Assessment Sheet
What Is the Task?
In the space provided, write what the assignment task is.

Strongest Paragraph
Tell the writer which paragraph you think is the strongest one, explaining specifically what makes it strong and accounting for how and where it responds effectively to the task and engages with the text(s).

Weakest Paragraph
Tell the writer which paragraph you think is the weakest one, explaining specifically what makes it weak and accounting for how and where it does not respond effectively to the task and/or disengages with the text(s).

What Is the Writer's Thesis?
Remember: a thesis statement is a narrow, argumentative assertion about a topic which forms the backbone of an essay. It alludes to evidence but does not necessarily "lay it all out" for the reader. The topic has to be questionable, meaning it can be argued. In other words, a thesis statement clearly states the writer's point of view but can still be argued by others. It opens up a debate, rather than shuts one down. Write below what you take to be the writer's thesis:

Reviewer's Name _____

■ Exercise
Peer Review #6: Project

Paper Author: _____

Instructions: Begin by reading the paper and making marginal and end comments. Try to make a comment about the project at the end of the introduction, and then a comment at the end of each paragraph reflecting on the success of that paragraph and the use of text. In the end comments, try to focus on what the author most needs to work on.

When you have finished commenting on the draft, complete this sheet.

Project

The project of a paper is its thesis or argument. It is the main point of the paper or what the paper is trying to achieve. Projects should engage both essays, should address the assignment on some level, and should be clearly evident in the introduction. Sometimes a paper's project is "emerging"—you can't find it in the intro, but you get a sense of it by the end of the paper. More solid projects will articulate what they are trying to do right up front. Projects that compare/contrast are not the strongest. The strongest projects are original, insightful, confident, and yet also aware of their own limitations. They don't claim too much or ignore evidence to make themselves work. Instead, they stake a very limited and provable claim.

In your own words, what is the project of this paper?

Find the sentence(s) in the introduction that state the project and place an asterisk there. If you cannot find such a statement of the project, place a large exclamation point next to the intro.

How could the author make this project more specific?

How could the author make this project more complex/complicated?

Text

There are three main textual protocols: reference, paraphrase, and quotation. Use reference if you just want to mention an incident in an essay ("When Tompkins looked at another source…"); use paraphrase (and a citation) when you want to paraphrase a statement from the essay; use quotation (and a citation) for passages that have important ideas, require some analysis, or are particularly important to your project. Quotation is one of the strongest textual protocols when pursuing a project, but it's crucial to *use* quotation and not just "have" it. Using quotation means that you retain its specificity as you move into your analysis or into the other text. To do that, apply the concepts from the quotation in detail or reuse pieces of the quotation in your later analysis.

Find the strongest use of quotation in the paper and put two plus signs next to it. What makes it strong?

Find the weakest use of text in general in the paper and put two minus signs next to it. How could it be made stronger?

Does every paragraph use at least one of the textual protocols? If no, place an exclamation point next to paragraphs that do not.

Organization

Strong organization means that every paragraph has a function in the pursuit of the project, and that function is made clear in the thesis statement. It also means that the transitions between the paragraphs create an overall flow to the paper and indicate the logical progression of the paper. Paragraphs that could be rearranged without altering the paper suggest a weak organization. Thesis statements that use "another," "one," "a," or "also" suggest possible weak organization.

Does the start of each paragraph clearly indicate what the actual paragraph talks about? Put a sad face ☹ next to any that do not.

Does each transition reflect an overall logical progression? Put a "T" next to paragraphs that need a better transition.

Mark the weakest paragraph with a "W." What makes it weak?

Reviewer's Name _____

■ Exercise

Peer Review #6: Project

Paper Author: _____

Instructions: Begin by reading the paper and making marginal and end comments. Try to make a comment about the project at the end of the introduction, and then a comment at the end of each paragraph reflecting on the success of that paragraph and the use of text. In the end comments, try to focus on what the author most needs to work on.

When you have finished commenting on the draft, complete this sheet.

Project

The project of a paper is its thesis or argument. It is the main point of the paper or what the paper is trying to achieve. Projects should engage both essays, should address the assignment on some level, and should be clearly evident in the introduction. Sometimes a paper's project is "emerging"—you can't find it in the intro, but you get a sense of it by the end of the paper. More solid projects will articulate what they are trying to do right up front. Projects that compare/contrast are not the strongest. The strongest projects are original, insightful, confident, and yet also aware of their own limitations. They don't claim too much or ignore evidence to make themselves work. Instead, they stake a very limited and provable claim.

In your own words, what is the project of this paper?

Find the sentence(s) in the introduction that state the project and place an asterisk there. If you cannot find such a statement of the project, place a large exclamation point next to the intro.

How could the author make this project more specific?

How could the author make this project more complex/complicated?

Text

There are three main textual protocols: reference, paraphrase, and quotation. Use reference if you just want to mention an incident in an essay ("When Tompkins looked at another source…"); use paraphrase (and a citation) when you want to paraphrase a statement from the essay; use quotation (and a citation) for passages that have important ideas, require some analysis, or are particularly important to your project. Quotation is one of the strongest textual protocols when pursuing a project, but it's crucial to *use* quotation and not just "have" it. Using quotation means that you retain its specificity as you move into your analysis or into the other text. To do that, apply the concepts from the quotation in detail or reuse pieces of the quotation in your later analysis.

Find the strongest use of quotation in the paper and put two plus signs next to it. What makes it strong?

Find the weakest use of text in general in the paper and put two minus signs next to it. How could it be made stronger?

Does every paragraph use at least one of the textual protocols? If no, place an exclamation point next to paragraphs that do not.

Organization

Strong organization means that every paragraph has a function in the pursuit of the project, and that function is made clear in the thesis statement. It also means that the transitions between the paragraphs create an overall flow to the paper and indicate the logical progression of the paper. Paragraphs that could be rearranged without altering the paper suggest a weak organization. Thesis statements that use "another," "one," "a," or "also" suggest possible weak organization.

Does the start of each paragraph clearly indicate what the actual paragraph talks about? Put a sad face ☹ next to any that do not.

Does each transition reflect an overall logical progression? Put a "T" next to paragraphs that need a better transition.

Mark the weakest paragraph with a "W." What makes it weak?

Reviewer's Name _____

■ Exercise

Peer Review #6: Project

Paper Author: _____

Instructions: Begin by reading the paper and making marginal and end comments. Try to make a comment about the project at the end of the introduction, and then a comment at the end of each paragraph reflecting on the success of that paragraph and the use of text. In the end comments, try to focus on what the author most needs to work on.

When you have finished commenting on the draft, complete this sheet.

Project

The project of a paper is its thesis or argument. It is the main point of the paper or what the paper is trying to achieve. Projects should engage both essays, should address the assignment on some level, and should be clearly evident in the introduction. Sometimes a paper's project is "emerging"—you can't find it in the intro, but you get a sense of it by the end of the paper. More solid projects will articulate what they are trying to do right up front. Projects that compare/contrast are not the strongest. The strongest projects are original, insightful, confident, and yet also aware of their own limitations. They don't claim too much or ignore evidence to make themselves work. Instead, they stake a very limited and provable claim.

In your own words, what is the project of this paper?

Find the sentence(s) in the introduction that state the project and place an asterisk there. If you cannot find such a statement of the project, place a large exclamation point next to the intro.

How could the author make this project more specific?

How could the author make this project more complex/complicated?

Text

There are three main textual protocols: reference, paraphrase, and quotation. Use reference if you just want to mention an incident in an essay ("When Tompkins looked at another source…"); use paraphrase (and a citation) when you want to paraphrase a statement from the essay; use quotation (and a citation) for passages that have important ideas, require some analysis, or are particularly important to your project. Quotation is one of the strongest textual protocols when pursuing a project, but it's crucial to *use* quotation and not just "have" it. Using quotation means that you retain its specificity as you move into your analysis or into the other text. To do that, apply the concepts from the quotation in detail or reuse pieces of the quotation in your later analysis.

Find the strongest use of quotation in the paper and put two plus signs next to it. What makes it strong?

Find the weakest use of text in general in the paper and put two minus signs next to it. How could it be made stronger?

Does every paragraph use at least one of the textual protocols? If no, place an exclamation point next to paragraphs that do not.

Organization

Strong organization means that every paragraph has a function in the pursuit of the project, and that function is made clear in the thesis statement. It also means that the transitions between the paragraphs create an overall flow to the paper and indicate the logical progression of the paper. Paragraphs that could be rearranged without altering the paper suggest a weak organization. Thesis statements that use "another," "one," "a," or "also" suggest possible weak organization.

Does the start of each paragraph clearly indicate what the actual paragraph talks about? Put a sad face ☹ next to any that do not.

Does each transition reflect an overall logical progression? Put a "T" next to paragraphs that need a better transition.

Mark the weakest paragraph with a "W." What makes it weak?

Reviewer's Name _____

■ Exercise
Peer Review #7: Project, Short Form

Paper Author: _____

Paper Title: _____

BEFORE YOU READ THROUGH THE PAPER, read ONLY the introduction and then copy the project here:

Now, from that project, sketch out what you think would be a logical outline of the paragraphs:

Read through the paper, making marginal and end comments as needed. Did the paper have the organization suggested by the project? If not, was the paper's organization better or worse, and why? All paragraphs should be idea-centered. Put an exclamation point next to paragraphs whose topic sentences suggest no connection, no relation to the thesis, remain trapped in the texts, or have no idea focus.

■ Exercise

Peer Review #7: Project, Short Form

Paper Author: _____

Paper Title: _____

BEFORE YOU READ THROUGH THE PAPER, read ONLY the introduction and then copy the project here:

Now, from that project, sketch out what you think would be a logical outline of the paragraphs:

Read through the paper, making marginal and end comments as needed. Did the paper have the organization suggested by the project? If not, was the paper's organization better or worse, and why? All paragraphs should be idea-centered. Put an exclamation point next to paragraphs whose topic sentences suggest no connection, no relation to the thesis, remain trapped in the texts, or have no idea focus.

Reviewer's Name _____

■ Exercise

Peer Review #7: Project, Short Form

Paper Author: _____

Paper Title: _____

BEFORE YOU READ THROUGH THE PAPER, read ONLY the introduction and then copy the project here:

Now, from that project, sketch out what you think would be a logical outline of the paragraphs:

Read through the paper, making marginal and end comments as needed. Did the paper have the organization suggested by the project? If not, was the paper's organization better or worse, and why? All paragraphs should be idea-centered. Put an exclamation point next to paragraphs whose topic sentences suggest no connection, no relation to the thesis, remain trapped in the texts, or have no idea focus.

Reviewer's Name _____

■ Exercise

Peer Review #8: Checklist!

Peer revision for: _____

Instructions: Use this checklist to perform a thorough peer review.

Section I: Introduction

1. Are the titles of both essays present and correctly spelled?

2. Are the full names of both authors present and correctly spelled?

3. Is the argument clear?

   Put an asterisk next to the argument. In the margins of the paper, comment on the argument. Is it debatable? Does it connect both essays? Is it specific? How could it be made better? Give suggestions for revising the argument.

4. Is the introduction "introductory"?

   Is it too brief? Too specific? What might improve it? Make comments in the margins on how to improve the introduction.

Section II: Body

1. Is this essay making connections?

   Put a "+" next to each connection. For each connection you find, use the following questions to help you make comments in the margins of the paper:

   a) Does the writer use quotations from both essays to make the connection? If not, can you suggest a quotation that will help the writer make that connection?

   b) Do you understand the connection being made?

   c) Is it clearly explained? Can you see the connection from their explanation of the quotes? Does the explanation use the quotations?

Section III: Details

1. Do you see any obvious typographical or spelling errors? Circle any errors you see. If you're not sure whether or not something is wrong, tell the writer to check it.

2. Is the paper long enough?

   If not, make suggestions on how to expand. Sometimes a good way to expand a paper is to add more connections, explain connections you have more completely, or locate new quotations to use. Do you think any of these strategies can help?

3. Is the paper well-organized?

   Were you able to follow the argument? If there was any place where the essay lost you, go back and put two asterisks next to it. Let the writer know what you found confusing about that part, or how it lost you. Suggest ways to reorganize.

4. Does the essay prove its argument?

Section IV: Other Suggestions

At the end of the paper, make general comments. Try to focus on two things: first, let the writer know what you think they are doing well (finding an argument, choosing quotations, making connections, explaining connections, etc.). Then, explain the ONE thing you think the writer REALLY needs to focus on to improve the paper.

Reviewer's Name _____

■ Exercise

Peer Review #8: Checklist!

Peer revision for: _____

Instructions: Use this checklist to perform a thorough peer review.

Section I: Introduction
1. Are the titles of both essays present and correctly spelled?

2. Are the full names of both authors present and correctly spelled?

3. Is the argument clear?

    Put an asterisk next to the argument. In the margins of the paper, comment on the argument. Is it debatable? Does it connect both essays? Is it specific? How could it be made better? Give suggestions for revising the argument.

4. Is the introduction "introductory"?

    Is it too brief? Too specific? What might improve it? Make comments in the margins on how to improve the introduction.

Section II: Body
1. Is this essay making connections?

    Put a "+" next to each connection. For each connection you find, use the following questions to help you make comments in the margins of the paper:

    a) Does the writer use quotations from both essays to make the connection? If not, can you suggest a quotation that will help the writer make that connection?

    b) Do you understand the connection being made?

    c) Is it clearly explained? Can you see the connection from their explanation of the quotes? Does the explanation use the quotations?

Section III: Details

1. Do you see any obvious typographical or spelling errors? Circle any errors you see. If you're not sure whether or not something is wrong, tell the writer to check it.

2. Is the paper long enough?

   If not, make suggestions on how to expand. Sometimes a good way to expand a paper is to add more connections, explain connections you have more completely, or locate new quotations to use. Do you think any of these strategies can help?

3. Is the paper well-organized?

   Were you able to follow the argument? If there was any place where the essay lost you, go back and put two asterisks next to it. Let the writer know what you found confusing about that part, or how it lost you. Suggest ways to reorganize.

4. Does the essay prove its argument?

Section IV: Other Suggestions

At the end of the paper, make general comments. Try to focus on two things: first, let the writer know what you think they are doing well (finding an argument, choosing quotations, making connections, explaining connections, etc.). Then, explain the ONE thing you think the writer REALLY needs to focus on to improve the paper.

Reviewer's Name _____

■ Exercise

Peer Review #8: Checklist!

Peer revision for: _____

Instructions: Use this checklist to perform a thorough peer review.

Section I: Introduction

1. Are the titles of both essays present and correctly spelled?

2. Are the full names of both authors present and correctly spelled?

3. Is the argument clear?

    Put an asterisk next to the argument. In the margins of the paper, comment on the argument. Is it debatable? Does it connect both essays? Is it specific? How could it be made better? Give suggestions for revising the argument.

4. Is the introduction "introductory"?

    Is it too brief? Too specific? What might improve it? Make comments in the margins on how to improve the introduction.

Section II: Body

1. Is this essay making connections?

    Put a "+" next to each connection. For each connection you find, use the following questions to help you make comments in the margins of the paper:

    a) Does the writer use quotations from both essays to make the connection? If not, can you suggest a quotation that will help the writer make that connection?

    b) Do you understand the connection being made?

    c) Is it clearly explained? Can you see the connection from their explanation of the quotes? Does the explanation use the quotations?

Section III: Details

1. Do you see any obvious typographical or spelling errors? Circle any errors you see. If you're not sure whether or not something is wrong, tell the writer to check it.

2. Is the paper long enough?

   If not, make suggestions on how to expand. Sometimes a good way to expand a paper is to add more connections, explain connections you have more completely, or locate new quotations to use. Do you think any of these strategies can help?

3. Is the paper well-organized?

   Were you able to follow the argument? If there was any place where the essay lost you, go back and put two asterisks next to it. Let the writer know what you found confusing about that part, or how it lost you. Suggest ways to reorganize.

4. Does the essay prove its argument?

Section IV: Other Suggestions

At the end of the paper, make general comments. Try to focus on two things: first, let the writer know what you think they are doing well (finding an argument, choosing quotations, making connections, explaining connections, etc.). Then, explain the ONE thing you think the writer REALLY needs to focus on to improve the paper.

Reviewer's Name _____

■ Exercise

Peer Review #9: Revision Project
by Elizabeth Kelly

Author: _____

Title: _____

Both the original paper and the revised paper are required for this review.

A. Introduction

1. Give the thesis of the original paper:

2. Give the thesis of the revision paper:

3. Is this thesis arguable? What would one opposing argument be?

4. What is the title of this paper?

5. Does the title accurately reflect the content of this paper?

6. What else should the author include in the introduction to make it clearer and draw you in as a reader?

B. Body Paragraphs: Write the topic sentence of each body paragraph first, then go back and fill in the appropriate blanks between your topic sentences with a phrase or sentence explaining the connection between the paragraphs. (Example: Body Paragraph one topic sentence: Our true selves express the basis for our human dignity. Connection 1: We lose our true selves because we cover. Paragraph 2: Covering our true selves leads to losing the basis for our human diginity)

Topic Sentence, 1st Body Paragraph:

Connection:
Topic Sentence, 2nd Body Paragraph:

Connection:
Topic Sentence, 3rd Body Paragraph:

Connection:
Topic Sentence, 4th Body Paragraph:

C. Conclusion

1. If this were the first chapter of a book, and you were writing the second, what would you write about?

2. What would the second chapter be called?

3. What would its thesis be?

D. Overall Argument—Draw the argument. (Does it circle back on itself? Is it linear or does it branch out?) Simple geometric representations are fine.

Give a brief explanation for the drawing you made:

E. Does this paper constitute a substantial revision of the original paper? What percent of the paper has been changed?

Reviewer's Name _____

■ Exercise

Peer Revision #9: Revision Project
by Elizabeth Kelly

Author: _____

Title: _____

Both the original paper and the revised paper are required for this review.

A. Introduction

1. Give the thesis of the original paper:

2. Give the thesis of the revision paper:

3. Is this thesis arguable? What would one opposing argument be?

4. What is the title of this paper?

5. Does the title accurately reflect the content of this paper?

6. What else should the author include in the introduction to make it clearer and draw you in as a reader?

B. Body Paragraphs: Write the topic sentence of each body paragraph first, then go back and fill in the appropriate blanks between your topic sentences with a phrase or sentence explaining the connection between the paragraphs. (Example: Body Paragraph one topic sentence: Our true selves express the basis for our human dignity. Connection 1: We lose our true selves because we cover. Paragraph 2: Covering our true selves leads to losing the basis for our human diginity)

Topic Sentence, 1st Body Paragraph:

Connection:
Topic Sentence, 2nd Body Paragraph:

Connection:
Topic Sentence, 3rd Body Paragraph:

Connection:
Topic Sentence, 4th Body Paragraph:

C. Conclusion

1. If this were the first chapter of a book, and you were writing the second, what would you write about?

2. What would the second chapter be called?

3. What would its thesis be?

D. Overall Argument—Draw the argument. (Does it circle back on itself? Is it linear or does it branch out?) Simple geometric representations are fine.

Give a brief explanation for the drawing you made:

E. Does this paper constitute a substantial revision of the original paper? What percent of the paper has been changed?

Reviewer's Name _____

■ Exercise

Peer Revision #9: Revision Project
by Elizabeth Kelly

Author: _____

Title: _____

Both the original paper and the revised paper are required for this review.

A. Introduction

1. Give the thesis of the original paper:

2. Give the thesis of the revision paper:

3. Is this thesis arguable? What would one opposing argument be?

4. What is the title of this paper?

5. Does the title accurately reflect the content of this paper?

6. What else should the author include in the introduction to make it clearer and draw you in as a reader?

B. Body Paragraphs: Write the topic sentence of each body paragraph first, then go back and fill in the appropriate blanks between your topic sentences with a phrase or sentence explaining the connection between the paragraphs. (Example: Body Paragraph one topic sentence: Our true selves express the basis for our human dignity. Connection 1: We lose our true selves because we cover. Paragraph 2: Covering our true selves leads to losing the basis for our human diginity)

Topic Sentence, 1st Body Paragraph:

Connection:
Topic Sentence, 2nd Body Paragraph:

Connection:
Topic Sentence, 3rd Body Paragraph:

Connection:
Topic Sentence, 4th Body Paragraph:

C. Conclusion

1. If this were the first chapter of a book, and you were writing the second, what would you write about?

2. What would the second chapter be called?

3. What would its thesis be?

D. Overall Argument—Draw the argument. (Does it circle back on itself? Is it linear or does it branch out?) Simple geometric representations are fine.

Give a brief explanation for the drawing you made:

E. Does this paper constitute a substantial revision of the original paper? What percent of the paper has been changed?

■ Exercise
Peer Review #10: Evaluation Criteria
by Jessica Murray-Cooke

Opening Paragraph

- Essay has a creative and original title.

- Opening sentence is original, unusual, or otherwise engaging.

- Provides a well-formulated and easily identifiable thesis statement.

Closing Paragraph

- Offers a conclusive, illuminating statement about the texts, rather than a simple summary.

- Ends on a skillful note, either by employing a theme throughout the work or by making a noteworthy closing comment.

Sentence Level Issues/Concerns

- Writer writes in a consistent medium to formal tone.

- Avoids contractions.

- Avoids the use of the second person.

- Writer uses proper MLA citation practices for in-text quotations.

- Writer includes a properly formatted works cited page.

- Writer creates effective transitions between sentences and paragraphs.

- Writer uses appropriate, informative, creative, and varied signal phrases to introduce and incorporate quoted material.

Close Reading, Critical Thinking, Analysis, and Synthesis
Organization

1. Indiscernible, unapparent—I cannot follow this paper's logic and/or order.

2. Unclear and ineffective—I have difficulty following this paper's logic and/or order. I may have a sense of the writer's purpose, but I'm not entirely sure where it's going.

3. Adequate—I'm pretty sure I can follow this paper's logic and/or order. The order and presentation of ideas is competent but not skillful.

4. Capable and proficient—I follow this paper's logic and/or order. The order and presentation of ideas is skillful, but not flawless

5. Successful—I know *exactly* what the writer's stance is and how the writer will argue the case (logic); plus, I know *exactly* where this essay is going (order).

Content

1. Sketchy, absent, rough, shallow—I neither see nor understand what the writer is trying to say about the texts or how the writer is responding to the task.

2. Vague, imprecise, overly broad—I have difficulty understanding what the writer is trying to say about the texts and/or how the writer is responding to the task.

3. Demonstrates general understanding of the text, though may not dig into it fully—I can see and understand what the writer is trying to say and how the writer is responding to the task, but I'm not fully convinced by the evidence yet.

4. Reveals understanding of the text and shows this off by offering thoughtful connections and analysis—It is easy to understand what the writer is trying to say and how the writer is responding to the task and working with the texts.

5. Rich, dense, thought-provoking, profound—It is effortless to see what the writer is saying and to identify how the writer responds to the task and engages with the texts.

Treatment of Subject

1. Novice—I feel like the writer does not understand the texts or the task (or both).

2. Elementary, simple—I feel like the writer needs to re-read the texts and the task.

3. Adequate—I feel like the way the writer wrote about the text and responded to the task provides me just enough material to keep me sustained from start to finish but not enough to make me want to reread it.

4. Skillful—I feel like the way the writer wrote about the texts and responded to the task provides more than enough material to keep me sustained. I may want to reread this essay.

5. Substantial—I feel like the way the writer wrote about the text and responded to the task provides loads of material to sustain me; keep me reading and thinking. I definitely want to reread this essay.

Writer's Tone

1. Indecisive, fluctuating, inconsistent—I have no idea where the writer stands on the texts and task.

2. Awkward and ambiguous—I have only a vague notion of where the writer stands on the texts and task.

3. Coherent, but not authoritative—I have a good idea where the writer stands on the text and task, but the writer's tone is neither convincing nor authoritative.

4. Convincing, but not necessarily commanding—I am feeling convinced about where the writer stands on the texts and task. This writer seems reasonably sure of herself/himself.

5. Authoritative—I know for sure where this writer stands on the texts and task because the writer is certain of herself/himself (without being overconfident).

Mechanical Errors

1. More than 12 per page; prohibits readability.

2. More than 5 but fewer than 12 per page; damages readability.

3. More than 5 per page; affects quality of readability, but does not damage it.

4. Fewer than 5 per page; has little to no impact on readability. The writer's style and flair are emerging as interesting elements of her/his writing.

5. Practically flawless; in fact, the writer uses grammar, mechanics, and sentence structure to enhance the work. The writer's style, diction, syntax, and flair are compelling elements of her/his writing.

Information Delivery

1. Missing—I didn't learn anything about the texts and the task from this author.

2. Insufficient—I didn't learn anything new about the texts and the task from this author.

3. Thin and commonplace—I learned a little about the texts and the task from this author, but the information presented is probably what most people would say.

4. Substantial in both quantity and quality—I feel like I learned something interesting about the texts and the task from this author. Moreover, the case made is more than what most people would say.

5. Substantial and substantive—I feel significantly taught by this author about the texts and the task. In addition, the case presented is unique, rich, and considerable.

Ideas

1. Shallow and undeveloped; feels like it's been written in haste, without preparation—I feel the writer missed the task and avoided engaging meaningfully with the texts.

2. One-dimensional and underdeveloped—I feel the writer either missed the task or avoided engaging meaningfully with the texts.

3. Straightforward and without expansion and/or maturity—I think the author could do and say more about the texts and the task if the writer builds upon and expands the ideas more.

4. Good quality—I can tell this author has given serious thought to the task and the texts.

5. Exceptional quality—I can see this author has given significant thought to the task and texts.

Second Reading Invitation?

I want to read this paper again because it is interesting, informative, engaging, coherent, cohesive, and educational to me about the text(s).

1. No

2. Yes

Enter Total Score Here: _____ (out of a possible 37)

1 – 14 Global Revision Recommendation

15 – 26 Conceptual Revision Recommendation

27 – 35 Local Revision Recommendation

36 – 37 No Revision Necessary

■ Exercise

Peer Review #10: Evaluation Criteria
by Jessica Murray-Cooke

Opening Paragraph

- Essay has a creative and original title
- Opening sentence is original, unusual, or otherwise engaging.
- Provides a well-formulated and easily identifiable thesis statement.

Closing Paragraph

- Offers a conclusive, illuminating statement about the texts, rather than a simple summary.
- Ends on a skillful note, either by employing a theme throughout the work or by making a noteworthy closing comment.

Sentence Level Issues/Concerns

- Writer writes in a consistent medium to formal tone.
- Avoids contractions.
- Avoids the use of the second person.
- Writer uses proper MLA citation practices for in-text quotations.
- Writer includes a properly formatted works cited page.
- Writer creates effective transitions between sentences and paragraphs.
- Writer uses appropriate, informative, creative, and varied signal phrases to introduce and incorporate quoted material.

Close Reading, Critical Thinking, Analysis, and Synthesis
Organization

1. Indiscernible, unapparent—I cannot follow this paper's logic and/or order.
2. Unclear and ineffective—I have difficulty following this paper's logic and/or order. I may have a sense of the writer's purpose, but I'm not entirely sure where it's going.
3. Adequate—I'm pretty sure I can follow this paper's logic and/or order. The order and presentation of ideas is competent but not skillful.
4. Capable and proficient—I follow this paper's logic and/or order. The order and presentation of ideas is skillful, but not flawless
5. Successful—I know *exactly* what the writer's stance is and how the writer will argue the case (logic); plus, I know *exactly* where this essay is going (order).

Content

1. Sketchy, absent, rough, shallow—I neither see nor understand what the writer is trying to say about the texts or how the writer is responding to the task.

2. Vague, imprecise, overly broad—I have difficulty understanding what the writer is trying to say about the texts and/or how the writer is responding to the task.

3. Demonstrates general understanding of the text, though may not dig into it fully—I can see and understand what the writer is trying to say and how the writer is responding to the task, but I'm not fully convinced by the evidence yet.

4. Reveals understanding of the text and shows this off by offering thoughtful connections and analysis—It is easy to understand what the writer is trying to say and how the writer is responding to the task and working with the texts.

5. Rich, dense, thought-provoking, profound—It is effortless to see what the writer is saying and to identify how the writer responds to the task and engages with the texts.

Treatment of Subject

1. Novice—I feel like the writer does not understand the texts or the task (or both).

2. Elementary, simple—I feel like the writer needs to re-read the texts and the task.

3. Adequate—I feel like the way the writer wrote about the text and responded to the task provides me just enough material to keep me sustained from start to finish but not enough to make me want to reread it.

4. Skillful—I feel like the way the writer wrote about the texts and responded to the task provides more than enough material to keep me sustained. I may want to reread this essay.

5. Substantial—I feel like the way the writer wrote about the text and responded to the task provides loads of material to sustain me; keep me reading and thinking. I definitely want to reread this essay.

Writer's Tone

1. Indecisive, fluctuating, inconsistent—I have no idea where the writer stands on the texts and task.

2. Awkward and ambiguous—I have only a vague notion of where the writer stands on the texts and task.

3. Coherent, but not authoritative—I have a good idea where the writer stands on the text and task, but the writer's tone is neither convincing nor authoritative.

4. Convincing, but not necessarily commanding—I am feeling convinced about where the writer stands on the texts and task. This writer seems reasonably sure of herself/himself.

5. Authoritative—I know for sure where this writer stands on the texts and task because the writer is certain of herself/himself (without being overconfident).

Mechanical Errors

1. More than 12 per page; prohibits readability.

2. More than 5 but fewer than 12 per page; damages readability.

3. More than 5 per page; affects quality of readability, but does not damage it.

4. Fewer than 5 per page; has little to no impact on readability. The writer's style and flair are emerging as interesting elements of her/his writing.

5. Practically flawless; in fact, the writer uses grammar, mechanics, and sentence structure to enhance the work. The writer's style, diction, syntax, and flair are compelling elements of her/his writing.

Information Delivery

1. Missing—I didn't learn anything about the texts and the task from this author.

2. Insufficient—I didn't learn anything new about the texts and the task from this author.

3. Thin and commonplace—I learned a little about the texts and the task from this author, but the information presented is probably what most people would say.

4. Substantial in both quantity and quality—I feel like I learned something interesting about the texts and the task from this author. Moreover, the case made is more than what most people would say.

5. Substantial and substantive—I feel significantly taught by this author about the texts and the task. In addition, the case presented is unique, rich, and considerable.

Ideas

1. Shallow and undeveloped; feels like it's been written in haste, without preparation—I feel the writer missed the task and avoided engaging meaningfully with the texts.

2. One-dimensional and underdeveloped—I feel the writer either missed the task or avoided engaging meaningfully with the texts.

3. Straightforward and without expansion and/or maturity—I think the author could do and say more about the texts and the task if the writer builds upon and expands the ideas more.

4. Good quality—I can tell this author has given serious thought to the task and the texts.

5. Exceptional quality—I can see this author has given significant thought to the task and texts.

Second Reading Invitation?

I want to read this paper again because it is interesting, informative, engaging, coherent, cohesive, and educational to me about the text(s).

1. No

2. Yes

Enter Total Score Here: _____ (out of a possible 37)

1 – 14 Global Revision Recommendation

15 – 26 Conceptual Revision Recommendation

27 – 35 Local Revision Recommendation

36 – 37 No Revision Necessary

■ Exercise

Peer Review #10: Evaluation Criteria
by Jessica Murray-Cooke

Opening Paragraph

- Essay has a creative and original title
- Opening sentence is original, unusual, or otherwise engaging.
- Provides a well-formulated and easily identifiable thesis statement.

Closing Paragraph

- Offers a conclusive, illuminating statement about the texts, rather than a simple summary.
- Ends on a skillful note, either by employing a theme throughout the work or by making a noteworthy closing comment.

Sentence Level Issues/Concerns

- Writer writes in a consistent medium to formal tone.
- Avoids contractions.
- Avoids the use of the second person.
- Writer uses proper MLA citation practices for in-text quotations.
- Writer includes a properly formatted works cited page.
- Writer creates effective transitions between sentences and paragraphs.
- Writer uses appropriate, informative, creative, and varied signal phrases to introduce and incorporate quoted material.

Close Reading, Critical Thinking, Analysis, and Synthesis

Organization

1. Indiscernible, unapparent—I cannot follow this paper's logic and/or order.
2. Unclear and ineffective—I have difficulty following this paper's logic and/or order. I may have a sense of the writer's purpose, but I'm not entirely sure where it's going.
3. Adequate—I'm pretty sure I can follow this paper's logic and/or order. The order and presentation of ideas is competent but not skillful.
4. Capable and proficient—I follow this paper's logic and/or order. The order and presentation of ideas is skillful, but not flawless
5. Successful—I know *exactly* what the writer's stance is and how the writer will argue the case (logic); plus, I know *exactly* where this essay is going (order).

Content

1. Sketchy, absent, rough, shallow—I neither see nor understand what the writer is trying to say about the texts or how the writer is responding to the task.

2. Vague, imprecise, overly broad—I have difficulty understanding what the writer is trying to say about the texts and/or how the writer is responding to the task.

3. Demonstrates general understanding of the text, though may not dig into it fully—I can see and understand what the writer is trying to say and how the writer is responding to the task, but I'm not fully convinced by the evidence yet.

4. Reveals understanding of the text and shows this off by offering thoughtful connections and analysis—It is easy to understand what the writer is trying to say and how the writer is responding to the task and working with the texts.

5. Rich, dense, thought-provoking, profound—It is effortless to see what the writer is saying and to identify how the writer responds to the task and engages with the texts.

Treatment of Subject

1. Novice—I feel like the writer does not understand the texts or the task (or both).

2. Elementary, simple—I feel like the writer needs to re-read the texts and the task.

3. Adequate—I feel like the way the writer wrote about the text and responded to the task provides me just enough material to keep me sustained from start to finish but not enough to make me want to reread it.

4. Skillful—I feel like the way the writer wrote about the texts and responded to the task provides more than enough material to keep me sustained. I may want to reread this essay.

5. Substantial—I feel like the way the writer wrote about the text and responded to the task provides loads of material to sustain me; keep me reading and thinking. I definitely want to reread this essay.

Writer's Tone

1. Indecisive, fluctuating, inconsistent—I have no idea where the writer stands on the texts and task.

2. Awkward and ambiguous—I have only a vague notion of where the writer stands on the texts and task.

3. Coherent, but not authoritative—I have a good idea where the writer stands on the text and task, but the writer's tone is neither convincing nor authoritative.

4. Convincing, but not necessarily commanding—I am feeling convinced about where the writer stands on the texts and task. This writer seems reasonably sure of herself/himself.

5. Authoritative—I know for sure where this writer stands on the texts and task because the writer is certain of herself/himself (without being overconfident).

Mechanical Errors

1. More than 12 per page; prohibits readability.

2. More than 5 but fewer than 12 per page; damages readability.

3. More than 5 per page; affects quality of readability, but does not damage it.

4. Fewer than 5 per page; has little to no impact on readability. The writer's style and flair are emerging as interesting elements of her/his writing.

5. Practically flawless; in fact, the writer uses grammar, mechanics, and sentence structure to enhance the work. The writer's style, diction, syntax, and flair are compelling elements of her/his writing.

Information Delivery

1. Missing—I didn't learn anything about the texts and the task from this author.

2. Insufficient—I didn't learn anything new about the texts and the task from this author.

3. Thin and commonplace—I learned a little about the texts and the task from this author, but the information presented is probably what most people would say.

4. Substantial in both quantity and quality—I feel like I learned something interesting about the texts and the task from this author. Moreover, the case made is more than what most people would say.

5. Substantial and substantive—I feel significantly taught by this author about the texts and the task. In addition, the case presented is unique, rich, and considerable.

Ideas

1. Shallow and undeveloped; feels like it's been written in haste, without preparation—I feel the writer missed the task and avoided engaging meaningfully with the texts.

2. One-dimensional and underdeveloped—I feel the writer either missed the task or avoided engaging meaningfully with the texts.

3. Straightforward and without expansion and/or maturity—I think the author could do and say more about the texts and the task if the writer builds upon and expands the ideas more.

4. Good quality—I can tell this author has given serious thought to the task and the texts.

5. Exceptional quality—I can see this author has given significant thought to the task and texts.

Second Reading Invitation?
I want to read this paper again because it is interesting, informative, engaging, coherent, cohesive, and educational to me about the text(s).

1. No

2. Yes

Enter Total Score Here: _____ (out of a possible 37)

1 – 14 Global Revision Recommendation

15 – 26 Conceptual Revision Recommendation

27 – 35 Local Revision Recommendation

36 – 37 No Revision Necessary

■ Exercise

Peer Review #11: Quick Assessment Sheet

by Jessica Murray-Cooke

Paper Author: _____

Step 1: Quick Assessment Sheet

Use coordinating numbers in the left-hand column to write feedback and suggestions for improvement directly on your peer's paper. Put your initials next to your comments.

	Opening Paragraph	Circle One
1	Essay has a creative and original title	Strongly Agree Agree Disagree Strongly Disagree
2	Opening sentence is original, unusual, or otherwise engaging.	Strongly Agree Agree Disagree Strongly Disagree
3	Provides a well-formulated and easily identifiable thesis statement that directly and clearly answers the assignment prompt question.	Strongly Agree Agree Disagree Strongly Disagree
	Closing Paragraph	**Circle One**
4	Offers a conclusive, illuminating statement about the texts as an extension of the thesis statement, rather than a simple summary of the points made and the evidence provided.	Strongly Agree Agree Disagree Strongly Disagree
5	Ends on a skillful note, either by employing a theme throughout the work or by repeating a symbol.	Strongly Agree Agree Disagree Strongly Disagree
	Sentence Level Issues	**Circle One**
6	Writer writes in a **consistent** medium to formal tone. Avoids contractions. Avoids the use of the second person.	Strongly Agree Agree Disagree Strongly Disagree
7	Writer properly and consistently punctuates the text title either by underlining it or italicizing it as appropriate.	Strongly Agree Agree Disagree Strongly Disagree
8	Writer creates effective transitional phrases and sentences between sentences and paragraphs.	Strongly Agree Agree Disagree Strongly Disagree
9	Writer uses appropriate, informative, creative, and varied signal phrases to introduce and incorporate quoted material. *(These should be italicized.)*	Strongly Agree Agree Disagree Strongly Disagree
10	Writer uses proper MLA citation practices for in-text quotations.	Strongly Agree Agree Disagree Strongly Disagree
11	Writer includes a properly formatted works cited page.	Strongly Agree Agree Disagree Strongly Disagree

Step 2: Thesis Assessment

What is the writer's thesis?—A thesis statement is a narrow, argumentative assertion about a topic which forms the backbone of an essay. It alludes to evidence but does not necessarily "lay it all out" for the reader. The topic has to be questionable, meaning it can be argued. In other words, a thesis statement clearly states the writer's point of view but can still be argued by others. It opens up a debate, rather than shuts one down.

Read your peer's highlighted thesis statement; then, answer the following questions.

Your instructor has given you an assignment sheet. Sum up the assignment in one sentence here.

_____

Does the thesis statement directly and clearly answer this assignment prompt question:

_____ Yes _____ No

If yes, go to Step 3.

If no, go directly to the draft's closing paragraph, re-read it, and return to this section. (Often in a draft of an essay, a thesis statement will emerge in a closing paragraph because the writer is finally warmed up and has thought through her ideas.) Is there a budding thesis statement in the closing paragraph that to some degree answers the assignment prompt question?

_____ Yes _____ No

If yes, underline what you take to be the writer's thesis in the closing paragraph; then, go to Step 3.

If no, automatically recommend a global revision, a visit to the University Center for Excellence in Writing, and/or a visit with the instructor.

Step 3: Thesis Development Assessment

In the space provided below, explain how you (as the reader) see that either what the writer (or you) have identified as the thesis does directly and clearly answer the assignment prompt.

_____

_____

Step 4, Part A: Textual Evidence and Analysis Assessment

What is the writer's evidence? There is a smart and effective three-step method[1] to effectively incorporate quotations into essays that make interpretive arguments.

- **Step One:** Before the writer cites from the literary text, the writer should set up the quotation with her own writing so the reader is not confused about the context of the quotation. (A sophisticated setup can also guide the reader into the writer's interpretation of the passage.)

[1]Adapted from "Using Textual Evidence" by Ben Slote at Allegheny College <webpub.allegheny.edu/dept/writingcenter/assignments/textualevidence.doc> Accessed Sunday, October 21, 2007.

- **Step Two:** Cite the passage. A writer should only quote a passage from the text that illustrates the point in that paragraph.

- **Step Three:** The writer should then follow his or her selected quotation with writing that analyzes the quotation, explaining how exactly the quotation suggests the point the writer means to make by quoting the passage in the first place and, thus, offers concrete support to the thesis statement.

On your peer's paper, look for every instance where the writer put **direct quotations in bold print**; then, continue on with the following:

When the writer follows the three-step method, indicate this on your peer's paper by putting a check mark next to the direct quotation.

When the writer does not follow the three-step method, indicate this on your peer's paper by putting an X next to the direct quotation and explain why you think the quoted material is NOT illustrative of the thesis and why you think the selected quotation either does not "seem to fit" the analytical situation or the analysis is simply inadequate.

Step 4, Part B: Analysis and Interpretation Quality Control

Overall, does the writer's underlined analysis and interpretation of his or her selected textual evidence directly and clearly support and promote the writer's thesis statement and, thus, offer up a convincing argument to you?

_____ Yes   _____ No

If yes, go to Step 5.

If no, explain where and how the analysis strikes you as weak and/or underdeveloped; recommend a global revision, a visit to the University Center for Excellence in Writing, and/or a visit with the course instructor.

Step 5: Strong Man, Weak Man

Strongest paragraph—Put a star next to the paragraph you think is the strongest one, and in the space below *explain specifically* what makes it strong to you (the reader) and describe how and where it responds effectively to the task and engages with the text(s).

_____

_____

_____

_____

_____

Weakest paragraph—Circle the entire paragraph you think is the weakest one, and in the space below *explain specifically* what makes it weak and describe how and where the writing **does not respond** effectively to the task and/or disengages with the text(s).

_____

_____

_____

_____

_____

Step 6: How Different Is This Revision from the Draft?
Looking at back at the draft version of this essay, how different is the revision from the draft? Circle the answer that best applies.

•   Very different—this is practically a whole new paper with **exceptional** development and extension from the draft

•   Fairly different—some writing remains similar to the draft, but there is **ample** development and extension from the draft

•   Somewhat different—a lot of this writing looks like the draft, but there is **some** development and extension from the draft

•   About the same—almost all of this writing is the same as the draft, and there is **almost no** development and extension from the draft

Move on to Step 7.

Step 7: Assignment Assessment

Taking the list of items below into consideration,
•   **higher order issues: thesis, organization, development, purpose, and audience**
•   **later order concerns: titles, openings, closings, integration of quoted material, style, readability, and sentence-level error**
to what degree of success does the writing respond to the assignment?

5.   **Extremely Successful**—A 5 means that the quality of the essay's Organization, Content, Treatment of Subject, Tone, Information Delivery, and Ideas *are all outstanding in every category*. The writing itself is almost error-free, highly stylized, and makes the reader feel thoroughly impressed and informed by the writer. This sort of essay is a page-turner, with the reader actively anticipating the conclusion and wanting to reread the essay in its entirety.

•   Local Revision Recommendation

4. **Very Successful**—A 4 means that the quality of the essay's Organization, Content, Treatment of Subject, Tone, Information Delivery, and Ideas *are all very good, and some (but not all) categories exceed the assignment's expectations.* The writing itself may have some recurring patterns of minor sentence level errors, a strong (but not stylized) writing voice, and makes the reader feel informed by the writer. This is the sort of essay that has the reader anticipating the conclusion and wanting to reread the essay in part, or perhaps in its entirety.

   • Low-End Conceptual Revision Recommendation

3. **Successful**—A 3 means that the quality of the essay's Organization, Content, Treatment of Subject, Tone, Information Delivery, and Ideas *are all good, and meet the expectations of the assignment, but do not exceed them.* Thus, some content areas may vary in terms of strength and quality. There may be minor (but acceptable) deficiencies in the logic/analysis as well as a few recurring patterns of minor sentence level errors. At the end of the paper, the reader feels that the essay has met the assignment's principal goals but has not surpassed them.

   • Conceptual Revision Recommendation

2. **Not Successful**—A 2 means that the quality of the essay's Organization, Content, Treatment of Subject, Tone, Information Delivery, and Ideas *do not adequately meet the expectations of the assignment.* There are large deficiencies in one or more of the following areas: the logic, the structure/pace of the argument, the selected textual support, and/or the critical analysis of the text. There may also be several to many recurring patterns of sentence level errors that negatively impact the reader's comprehension of the writing. At the end of the paper, the reader feels that the essay has missed the assignment's goals and would substantially benefit from a major overhaul, such as a high-end conceptual revision or a global revision.

   • High-End Conceptual Revision and UCEW Visit Recommendation

   or

   • Global Revision and UCEW Visit Recommendation

1. **Not Successful At All**—A 1 means that the quality of the essay's Organization, Content, Treatment of Subject, Tone, Information Delivery, and Ideas *fail to meet the expectations of the assignment.* There are inexplicably large deficiencies in one or more of the following areas: the logic, the structure/pace of the argument, the selected textual support, and/or the critical analysis of the text. There may also be several to many recurring patterns of sentence level errors which negatively impact the reader's comprehension of the writing in addition to clear evidence of lack of editing and proofreading. At the end of the paper, the reader feels that the essay has missed the assignment's goals and was likely written in haste.

   • Global Revision and UCEW Visit Recommendation

Reviewer's Name _____

■ Exercise

Peer Review #11: Quick Assessment Sheet

by Jessica Murray-Cooke

Paper Author: _____

Step 1: Quick Assessment Sheet

Use coordinating numbers in the left-hand column to write feedback and suggestions for improvement directly on your peer's paper. Put your initials next to your comments.

	Opening Paragraph	Circle One
1	Essay has a creative and original title	Strongly Agree Agree Disagree Strongly Disagree
2	Opening sentence is original, unusual, or otherwise engaging.	Strongly Agree Agree Disagree Strongly Disagree
3	Provides a well-formulated and easily identifiable thesis statement that directly and clearly answers the assignment prompt question.	Strongly Agree Agree Disagree Strongly Disagree
	Closing Paragraph	**Circle One**
4	Offers a conclusive, illuminating statement about the texts as an extension of the thesis statement, rather than a simple summary of the points made and the evidence provided.	Strongly Agree Agree Disagree Strongly Disagree
5	Ends on a skillful note, either by employing a theme throughout the work or by repeating a symbol.	Strongly Agree Agree Disagree Strongly Disagree
	Sentence Level Issues	**Circle One**
6	Writer writes in a **consistent** medium to formal tone. Avoids contractions. Avoids the use of the second person.	Strongly Agree Agree Disagree Strongly Disagree
7	Writer properly and consistently punctuates the text title either by underlining it or italicizing it as appropriate.	Strongly Agree Agree Disagree Strongly Disagree
8	Writer creates effective transitional phrases and sentences between sentences and paragraphs.	Strongly Agree Agree Disagree Strongly Disagree
9	Writer uses appropriate, informative, creative, and varied signal phrases to introduce and incorporate quoted material. *(These should be italicized.)*	Strongly Agree Agree Disagree Strongly Disagree
10	Writer uses proper MLA citation practices for in-text quotations.	Strongly Agree Agree Disagree Strongly Disagree
11	Writer includes a properly formatted works cited page.	Strongly Agree Agree Disagree Strongly Disagree

Step 2: Thesis Assessment

What is the writer's thesis?—A thesis statement is a narrow, argumentative assertion about a topic which forms the backbone of an essay. It alludes to evidence but does not necessarily "lay it all out" for the reader. The topic has to be questionable, meaning it can be argued. In other words, a thesis statement clearly states the writer's point of view but can still be argued by others. It opens up a debate, rather than shuts one down.

Read your peer's highlighted thesis statement; then, answer the following questions.

Your instructor has given you an assignment sheet. Sum up the assignment in one sentence here.

_____

Does the thesis statement directly and clearly answer this assignment prompt question:

_____ Yes _____ No

If yes, go to Step 3.

If no, go directly to the draft's closing paragraph, re-read it, and return to this section. (Often in a draft of an essay, a thesis statement will emerge in a closing paragraph because the writer is finally warmed up and has thought through her ideas.) Is there a budding thesis statement in the closing paragraph that to some degree answers the assignment prompt question?

_____ Yes _____ No

If yes, underline what you take to be the writer's thesis in the closing paragraph; then, go to Step 3.

If no, automatically recommend a global revision, a visit to the University Center for Excellence in Writing, and/or a visit with the instructor.

Step 3: Thesis Development Assessment

In the space provided below, explain how you (as the reader) see that either what the writer (or you) have identified as the thesis does directly and clearly answer the assignment prompt.

_____

_____

Step 4, Part A: Textual Evidence and Analysis Assessment

What is the writer's evidence? There is a smart and effective three-step method[1] to effectively incorporate quotations into essays that make interpretive arguments.

- **Step One:** Before the writer cites from the literary text, the writer should set up the quotation with her own writing so the reader is not confused about the context of the quotation. (A sophisticated setup can also guide the reader into the writer's interpretation of the passage.)

[1]Adapted from "Using Textual Evidence" by Ben Slote at Allegheny College <webpub.allegheny.edu/dept/writingcenter/ assignments/textualevidence.doc> Accessed Sunday, October 21, 2007.

- **Step Two:** Cite the passage. A writer should only quote a passage from the text that illustrates the point in that paragraph.

- **Step Three:** The writer should then follow his or her selected quotation with writing that analyzes the quotation, explaining how exactly the quotation suggests the point the writer means to make by quoting the passage in the first place and, thus, offers concrete support to the thesis statement.

On your peer's paper, look for every instance where the writer put **direct quotations in bold print**; then, continue on with the following:

When the writer follows the three-step method, indicate this on your peer's paper by putting a check mark next to the direct quotation.

When the writer does not follow the three-step method, indicate this on your peer's paper by putting an X next to the direct quotation and explain why you think the quoted material is NOT illustrative of the thesis and why you think the selected quotation either does not "seem to fit" the analytical situation or the analysis is simply inadequate.

Step 4, Part B: Analysis and Interpretation Quality Control

Overall, does the writer's underlined analysis and interpretation of his or her selected textual evidence directly and clearly support and promote the writer's thesis statement and, thus, offer up a convincing argument to you?

_____ Yes   _____ No

If yes, go to Step 5.

If no, explain where and how the analysis strikes you as weak and/or underdeveloped; recommend a global revision, a visit to the University Center for Excellence in Writing, and/or a visit with the course instructor.

Step 5: Strong Man, Weak Man

Strongest paragraph—Put a star next to the paragraph you think is the strongest one, and in the space below *explain specifically* what makes it strong to you (the reader) and describe how and where it responds effectively to the task and engages with the text(s).

_____

_____

_____

_____

_____

Weakest paragraph—Circle the entire paragraph you think is the weakest one, and in the space below *explain specifically* what makes it weak and describe how and where the writing **does not respond** effectively to the task and/or disengages with the text(s).

_____

_____

_____

_____

_____

Step 6: How Different Is This Revision from the Draft?

Looking at back at the draft version of this essay, how different is the revision from the draft? Circle the answer that best applies.

- Very different—this is practically a whole new paper with **exceptional** development and extension from the draft

- Fairly different—some writing remains similar to the draft, but there is **ample** development and extension from the draft

- Somewhat different—a lot of this writing looks like the draft, but there is **some** development and extension from the draft

- About the same—almost all of this writing is the same as the draft, and there is **almost no** development and extension from the draft

Move on to Step 7.

Step 7: Assignment Assessment

Taking the list of items below into consideration,
- **higher order issues: thesis, organization, development, purpose, and audience**
- **later order concerns: titles, openings, closings, integration of quoted material, style, readability, and sentence-level error,**

to what degree of success does the writing respond to the assignment?

5. **Extremely Successful**—A 5 means that the quality of the essay's Organization, Content, Treatment of Subject, Tone, Information Delivery, and Ideas *are all outstanding in every category*. The writing itself is almost error-free, highly stylized, and makes the reader feel thoroughly impressed and informed by the writer. This sort of essay is a page-turner, with the reader actively anticipating the conclusion and wanting to reread the essay in its entirety.

- Local Revision Recommendation

4. **Very Successful**—A 4 means that the quality of the essay's Organization, Content, Treatment of Subject, Tone, Information Delivery, and Ideas *are all very good, and some (but not all) categories exceed the assignment's expectations.* The writing itself may have some recurring patterns of minor sentence level errors, a strong (but not stylized) writing voice, and makes the reader feel informed by the writer. This is the sort of essay that has the reader anticipating the conclusion and wanting to reread the essay in part, or perhaps in its entirety.

   • Low-End Conceptual Revision Recommendation

3. **Successful**—A 3 means that the quality of the essay's Organization, Content, Treatment of Subject, Tone, Information Delivery, and Ideas *are all good, and meet the expectations of the assignment, but do not exceed them.* Thus, some content areas may vary in terms of strength and quality. There may be minor (but acceptable) deficiencies in the logic/analysis as well as a few recurring patterns of minor sentence level errors. At the end of the paper, the reader feels that the essay has met the assignment's principal goals but has not surpassed them.

   • Conceptual Revision Recommendation

2. **Not Successful**—A 2 means that the quality of the essay's Organization, Content, Treatment of Subject, Tone, Information Delivery, and Ideas *do not adequately meet the expectations of the assignment.* There are large deficiencies in one or more of the following areas: the logic, the structure/pace of the argument, the selected textual support, and/or the critical analysis of the text. There may also be several to many recurring patterns of sentence level errors that negatively impact the reader's comprehension of the writing. At the end of the paper, the reader feels that the essay has missed the assignment's goals and would substantially benefit from a major overhaul, such as a high-end conceptual revision or a global revision.

   • High-End Conceptual Revision and UCEW Visit Recommendation

   or

   • Global Revision and UCEW Visit Recommendation

1. **Not Successful At All**—A 1 means that the quality of the essay's Organization, Content, Treatment of Subject, Tone, Information Delivery, and Ideas *fail to meet the expectations of the assignment.* There are inexplicably large deficiencies in one or more of the following areas: the logic, the structure/pace of the argument, the selected textual support, and/or the critical analysis of the text. There may also be several to many recurring patterns of sentence level errors which negatively impact the reader's comprehension of the writing in addition to clear evidence of lack of editing and proofreading. At the end of the paper, the reader feels that the essay has missed the assignment's goals and was likely written in haste.

   • Global Revision and UCEW Visit Recommendation

Section 6

Reviewer's Name _____

■ Exercise

Peer Review #11: Quick Assessment Sheet

by Jessica Murray-Cooke

Paper Author: _____

Step 1: Quick Assessment Sheet

Use coordinating numbers in the left-hand column to write feedback and suggestions for improvement directly on your peer's paper. Put your initials next to your comments.

	Opening Paragraph	Circle One
1	Essay has a creative and original title	Strongly Agree Agree Disagree Strongly Disagree
2	Opening sentence is original, unusual, or otherwise engaging.	Strongly Agree Agree Disagree Strongly Disagree
3	Provides a well-formulated and easily identifiable thesis statement that directly and clearly answers the assignment prompt question.	Strongly Agree Agree Disagree Strongly Disagree
	Closing Paragraph	**Circle One**
4	Offers a conclusive, illuminating statement about the texts as an extension of the thesis statement, rather than a simple summary of the points made and the evidence provided.	Strongly Agree Agree Disagree Strongly Disagree
5	Ends on a skillful note, either by employing a theme throughout the work or by repeating a symbol.	Strongly Agree Agree Disagree Strongly Disagree
	Sentence Level Issues	**Circle One**
6	Writer writes in a **consistent** medium to formal tone. Avoids contractions. Avoids the use of the second person.	Strongly Agree Agree Disagree Strongly Disagree
7	Writer properly and consistently punctuates the text title either by underlining it or italicizing it as appropriate.	Strongly Agree Agree Disagree Strongly Disagree
8	Writer creates effective transitional phrases and sentences between sentences and paragraphs.	Strongly Agree Agree Disagree Strongly Disagree
9	Writer uses appropriate, informative, creative, and varied signal phrases to introduce and incorporate quoted material. *(These should be italicized.)*	Strongly Agree Agree Disagree Strongly Disagree
10	Writer uses proper MLA citation practices for in-text quotations.	Strongly Agree Agree Disagree Strongly Disagree
11	Writer includes a properly formatted works cited page.	Strongly Agree Agree Disagree Strongly Disagree

Step 2: Thesis Assessment

What is the writer's thesis?—A thesis statement is a narrow, argumentative assertion about a topic which forms the backbone of an essay. It alludes to evidence but does not necessarily "lay it all out" for the reader. The topic has to be questionable, meaning it can be argued. In other words, a thesis statement clearly states the writer's point of view but can still be argued by others. It opens up a debate, rather than shuts one down.

Read your peer's highlighted thesis statement; then, answer the following questions.

Your instructor has given you an assignment sheet. Sum up the assignment in one sentence here.

_____

Does the thesis statement directly and clearly answer this assignment prompt question:

_____ Yes _____ No

If yes, go to Step 3.

If no, go directly to the draft's closing paragraph, re-read it, and return to this section. (Often in a draft of an essay, a thesis statement will emerge in a closing paragraph because the writer is finally warmed up and has thought through her ideas.) Is there a budding thesis statement in the closing paragraph that to some degree answers the assignment prompt question?

_____ Yes _____ No

If yes, underline what you take to be the writer's thesis in the closing paragraph; then, go to Step 3.

If no, automatically recommend a global revision, a visit to the University Center for Excellence in Writing, and/or a visit with the instructor.

Step 3: Thesis Development Assessment

In the space provided below, explain how you (as the reader) see that either what the writer (or you) have identified as the thesis does directly and clearly answer the assignment prompt.

_____

_____

Step 4, Part A: Textual Evidence and Analysis Assessment

What is the writer's evidence? There is a smart and effective three-step method[1] to effectively incorporate quotations into essays that make interpretive arguments.

- **Step One:** Before the writer cites from the literary text, the writer should set up the quotation with her own writing so the reader is not confused about the context of the quotation. (A sophisticated setup can also guide the reader into the writer's interpretation of the passage.)

[1]Adapted from "Using Textual Evidence" by Ben Slote at Allegheny College <webpub.allegheny.edu/dept/writingcenter/ assignments/textualevidence.doc> Accessed Sunday, October 21, 2007.

- **Step Two:** Cite the passage. A writer should only quote a passage from the text that illustrates the point in that paragraph.

- **Step Three:** The writer should then follow his or her selected quotation with writing that analyzes the quotation, explaining how exactly the quotation suggests the point the writer means to make by quoting the passage in the first place and, thus, offers concrete support to the thesis statement.

On your peer's paper, look for every instance where the writer put **direct quotations in bold print**; then, continue on with the following:

When the writer follows the three-step method, indicate this on your peer's paper by putting a check mark next to the direct quotation.

When the writer does not follow the three-step method, indicate this on your peer's paper by putting an X next to the direct quotation and explain why you think the quoted material is NOT illustrative of the thesis and why you think the selected quotation either does not "seem to fit" the analytical situation or the analysis is simply inadequate.

Step 4, Part B: Analysis and Interpretation Quality Control

Overall, does the writer's underlined analysis and interpretation of his or her selected textual evidence directly and clearly support and promote the writer's thesis statement and, thus, offer up a convincing argument to you?

_____ Yes   _____ No

If yes, go to Step 5.

If no, explain where and how the analysis strikes you as weak and/or underdeveloped; recommend a global revision, a visit to the University Center for Excellence in Writing, and/or a visit with the course instructor.

Step 5: Strong Man, Weak Man

Strongest paragraph—Put a star next to the paragraph you think is the strongest one, and in the space below *explain specifically* what makes it strong to you (the reader) and describe how and where it responds effectively to the task and engages with the text(s).

_____

_____

_____

_____

_____

Weakest paragraph—Circle the entire paragraph you think is the weakest one, and in the space below *explain specifically* what makes it weak and describe how and where the writing **does not respond** effectively to the task and/or disengages with the text(s).

_____

_____

_____

_____

_____

Step 6: How Different Is This Revision from the Draft?
Looking at back at the draft version of this essay, how different is the revision from the draft? Circle the answer that best applies.

• Very different—this is practically a whole new paper with **exceptional** development and extension from the draft

• Fairly different—some writing remains similar to the draft, but there is **ample** development and extension from the draft

• Somewhat different—a lot of this writing looks like the draft, but there is **some** development and extension from the draft

• About the same—almost all of this writing is the same as the draft, and there is **almost no** development and extension from the draft

Move on to Step 7.

Step 7: Assignment Assessment

Taking the list of items below into consideration,
• **higher order issues: thesis, organization, development, purpose, and audience**
• **later order concerns: titles, openings, closings, integration of quoted material, style, readability, and sentence-level error,**
to what degree of success does the writing respond to the assignment?

5. **Extremely Successful**—A 5 means that the quality of the essay's Organization, Content, Treatment of Subject, Tone, Information Delivery, and Ideas *are all outstanding in every category*. The writing itself is almost error-free, highly stylized, and makes the reader feel thoroughly impressed and informed by the writer. This sort of essay is a page-turner, with the reader actively anticipating the conclusion and wanting to reread the essay in its entirety.

    • Local Revision Recommendation

4. **Very Successful**—A 4 means that the quality of the essay's Organization, Content, Treatment of Subject, Tone, Information Delivery, and Ideas *are all very good, and some (but not all) categories exceed the assignment's expectations.* The writing itself may have some recurring patterns of minor sentence level errors, a strong (but not stylized) writing voice, and makes the reader feel informed by the writer. This is the sort of essay that has the reader anticipating the conclusion and wanting to reread the essay in part, or perhaps in its entirety.

    *   Low-End Conceptual Revision Recommendation

3. **Successful**—A 3 means that the quality of the essay's Organization, Content, Treatment of Subject, Tone, Information Delivery, and Ideas *are all good, and meet the expectations of the assignment, but do not exceed them.* Thus, some content areas may vary in terms of strength and quality. There may be minor (but acceptable) deficiencies in the logic/analysis as well as a few recurring patterns of minor sentence level errors. At the end of the paper, the reader feels that the essay has met the assignment's principal goals but has not surpassed them.

    *   Conceptual Revision Recommendation

2. **Not Successful**—A 2 means that the quality of the essay's Organization, Content, Treatment of Subject, Tone, Information Delivery, and Ideas *do not adequately meet the expectations of the assignment.* There are large deficiencies in one or more of the following areas: the logic, the structure/pace of the argument, the selected textual support, and/or the critical analysis of the text. There may also be several to many recurring patterns of sentence level errors that negatively impact the reader's comprehension of the writing. At the end of the paper, the reader feels that the essay has missed the assignment's goals and would substantially benefit from a major overhaul, such as a high-end conceptual revision or a global revision.

    *   High-End Conceptual Revision and UCEW Visit Recommendation

        or

    *   Global Revision and UCEW Visit Recommendation

1. **Not Successful At All**—A 1 means that the quality of the essay's Organization, Content, Treatment of Subject, Tone, Information Delivery, and Ideas *fail to meet the expectations of the assignment.* There are inexplicably large deficiencies in one or more of the following areas: the logic, the structure/pace of the argument, the selected textual support, and/or the critical analysis of the text. There may also be several to many recurring patterns of sentence level errors which negatively impact the reader's comprehension of the writing in addition to clear evidence of lack of editing and proofreading. At the end of the paper, the reader feels that the essay has missed the assignment's goals and was likely written in haste.

    *   Global Revision and UCEW Visit Recommendation

Reviewer's Name _____

■ Exercise

Peer Review #12: Peer Review Packet
Looking at a Draft
by Jessica Murray-Cooke

Author Name: _____

Step 1: Thesis Assessment

What is the writer's thesis?—A thesis statement is a narrow, argumentative assertion about a topic which forms the backbone of an essay. It alludes to evidence but does not necessarily "lay it all out" for the reader. The topic has to be questionable, meaning it can be argued. In other words, a thesis statement clearly states the writer's point of view but can still be argued by others. It opens up a debate, rather than shuts one down.

On your peer's paper, underline what you take to be the writer's thesis; then, answer the following questions.

Does the thesis statement directly and clearly answer this assignment prompt question: "Looking at Amir and applying your understanding of Phillips' theory to Amir, how do you assess this character? Is Phillips' work applicable, and more to the point, is the adult Amir a failure or a success?"

_____ Yes   _____ No

- **If yes,** go to Step 2.

- **If no,** go directly to the draft's closing paragraph. (Often in a draft of an essay, a thesis statement will emerge in a closing paragraph because the writer is finally warmed up and has thought through her ideas.) Is there a budding thesis statement in the closing paragraph that to some degree answers the assignment prompt question above?

_____ Yes   _____ No

- **If yes,** underline what you take to be the writer's thesis; then, go to Step 2.

- **If no,** automatically recommend a global revision, a visit to the University Center for Excellence in Writing, and/or a visit with the instructor.

Step 2: Textual Evidence and Analysis Assessment

What is the writer's evidence?—There is a smart and effective three-step method[1] to incorporate quotations into essays that make interpretive arguments.

- **Step One:** Before the writer cites from the literary text, the writer should set up the quotation with her own writing so the reader is not confused about the context of the quotation. (A sophisticated setup can also guide the reader into the writer's interpretation of the passage.)

[1]Adapted from "Using Textual Evidence" by Ben Slote at Allegheny College <webpub.allegheny.edu/dept/writingcenter/assignments/textualevidence.doc> Accessed Sunday, October 21, 2007.

- **Step Two:** Cite the passage. A writer should only quote a passage from the text that illustrates the point in that paragraph.

- **Step Three:** The writer should then follow her selected quotation with writing that analyzes the quotation, explaining how exactly the quotation suggests the point the writer means to make by quoting the passage in the first place and, thus, offers concrete support to the thesis statement.

On your peer's paper, circle every use of direct textual evidence; then, answer the following questions.

In the direct textual evidence circled, does the writer follow the three-step method to incorporate quotations as outlined above?

- **If yes,** indicate on your peer's paper every instance when the writer followed the three-step method and explain how the quoted material helps you understand the writer's thesis.

- **If no,** indicate on your peer's paper every instance when the writer did not follow the three-step method and explain how the quoted material does not help you understand the writer's thesis or why the quotation does not "seem to fit."

Overall, does the writer's selected textual evidence directly and clearly support the writer's thesis statement?

_____ Yes   _____ No

- **If yes,** go to Step 3.

- **If no,** recommend a global revision, a visit to the University Center for Excellence in Writing and/ or a visit with the course instructor.

Step 3: Close Reading, Critical Thinking, Analysis, and Synthesis Evaluation

Directions: Circle the number that best corresponds to your assessment of the writing elements identified below. At the end, tally the total number of points and offer a revision type. Remember, empty praise is just that: empty. If all you do as a reviewer is say, "Nice job!" you haven't really kept up your end of the peer review bargain.

Organization—the order that the ideas are presented in and the logic (or "flow") used to present them

1. Indiscernible, unapparent—I cannot follow this paper's logic and/or order.

2. Unclear and ineffective—I have difficulty following this paper's logic and/or order. I may have a sense of the writer's purpose, but I'm not entirely sure where it's going.

3. Adequate—I'm pretty sure I can follow this paper's logic and/or order. The order and presentation of ideas is competent but not skillful.

4. Capable and proficient—I follow this paper's logic and/or order. The order and presentation of ideas is skillful, but not flawless

5. Successful—I know *exactly* what the writer's stance is and how the writer will argue the case (logic); plus, I know *exactly* where this essay is going (order).

Content—the intrinsic quality or depth of the ideas presented

1. Sketchy, absent, rough, shallow—I neither see nor understand what the writer is trying to say about the texts or how the writer is responding to the task.

2. Vague, imprecise, overly broad—I have difficulty understanding what the writer is trying to say about the texts and/or how the writer is responding to the task.

3. Okay, broad, sometimes unspecific—I can see and understand what the writer is trying to say and how the writer is responding to the task, but I'm not fully convinced by the evidence yet. (This essay demonstrates general understanding of the text and task, though the analysis may not dig in with it fully and the response may not cover the task comprehensively.)

4. Good, interesting, revealing—It is easy to understand what the writer is trying to say and how the writer is responding to the task and working with the texts. (This essay reveals a developed understanding of the text and shows this off by offering thoughtful connections and analysis.)

5. Awesome, rich, dense, thought-provoking, profound—It is effortless to see what the writer is saying and to identify how the writer responds to the task and engages with the texts. (This essay showcases a mature and thorough comprehension of the text and an advanced level of analysis.)

Treatment of Subject—the writer's demonstration of his or her comprehension of the text and the task

1. Novice—I feel like the writer does not understand the texts or the task (or both).

2. Elementary, simple—I feel like the writer needs to re-read the texts and the task.

3. Adequate—I feel like the way the writer wrote about the text and responded to the task provides me just enough material to keep me sustained from start to finish but not enough to make me want to reread it.

4. Skillful—I feel like the way the writer wrote about the texts and responded to the task provides more than enough material to keep me sustained. I may want to reread this essay.

5. Sophisticated—I feel like the way the writer wrote about the text and responded to the task provides loads of material to sustain me; keep me reading and thinking. I definitely want to reread this essay.

Writer's Ethos—the reader's sense of the writer's level of authority over the text and the task

1. Indecisive, fluctuating, inconsistent—I have no idea where the writer stands on the texts and task.

2. Awkward and ambiguous—I have only a vague notion of where the writer stands on the texts and task.

3. Coherent, but not authoritative—I have a good idea where the writer stands on the text and task, but the writer's tone is neither convincing nor authoritative.

4. Convincing, but not necessarily commanding—I am feeling convinced about where the writer stands on the texts and task. This writer seems reasonably sure of herself/himself.

5. Authoritative—I know for sure where this writer stands on the texts and task because the writer is certain of herself/himself (without being overconfident).

Mechanical Errors—issues related to grammar, mechanics, editing, and proofreading

1. More than 12 per page; prohibits readability.

2. More than 5 but fewer than 12 per page; damages readability.

3. More than 5 per page; affects quality of readability, but does not damage it.

4. Fewer than 5 per page; has little to no impact on readability. The writer's style and flair are emerging as interesting elements of her/his writing.

5. Practically flawless; in fact, the writer uses grammar, mechanics, and sentence structure to enhance the work. The writer's style, diction, syntax, and flair are compelling elements of her/his writing.

Information Delivery—the level of the work's "teaching quality"

1. Missing—I didn't learn anything about the texts and the task from this author.

2. Insufficient—I didn't learn anything new about the texts and the task from this author.

3. Thin and commonplace—I learned a little about the texts and the task from this author, but the information presented is probably what most people would say.

4. Substantial in both quantity and quality—I feel like I learned something interesting about the texts and the task from this author. Moreover, the case made is more than what most people would say.

5. Substantial and substantive—I feel significantly taught by this author about the texts and the task. In addition, the case presented is unique, rich, and considerable.

Ideas—the core thinking which lays the foundation for the work overall

1. Shallow and undeveloped; feels like it's been written in haste, without preparation—I feel the writer missed the task and avoided engaging meaningfully with the texts.

2. One-dimensional and underdeveloped—I feel the writer either missed the task or avoided engaging meaningfully with the texts.

3. Straightforward and without expansion and/or maturity—I think the author could do and say more about the texts and the task if the writer builds upon and expands the ideas more.

4. Good quality—I can tell this author has given serious thought to the task and the texts.

5. Exceptional quality—I can see this author has given significant thought to the task and texts.

Second Reading Invitation?

I want to read this paper again because it is interesting, informative, engaging, coherent, cohesive, and educational to me about the text(s).

1. No

2. Yes

Enter Total Score Here: _____ (out of a possible 37)

1 – 14 Global Revision Recommendation

15 – 26 Conceptual Revision Recommendation

27 – 35 Local Revision Recommendation

36 – 37 No Revision Necessary

Three Types of Revisions

Check off your revision type suggestion.

Global Revision

- Writing does not respond to the task
- Ideas are underdeveloped and/or weak and/or biased
- Organization is unclear and/or ineffective
- Argument logic is unsound and/or untraceable
- Content is superficial and/or contains factual errors
- Writing style, format, and presentation are incomplete

Required Corrections

- ❏ Major overhaul of the paper
- ❏ 70–100% rewrite
- ❏ Sections and paragraphs rewritten, rearranged, added, and/or scrapped
- ❏ Retained sections and paragraphs elaborated, qualified, and/or extended

Conceptual Revision

- Writing responds to the task unsuccessfully and/or incompletely
- Ideas show signs of incomplete development
- Organization is ineffective and/or unobvious
- Argument logic is weak and/or biased and/or unrefined
- Content is casual and/or clumsy
- Writing style, format, and presentation are unpolished

Required Corrections

- ❏ Ideas worth keeping and rethinking
- ❏ Prose needs rewriting
- ❏ 45–70% rewrite
- ❏ Crafts a new response to the prompt with the same ideas
- ❏ Sections and paragraphs rewritten, rearranged, added, and/or scrapped
- ❏ Ideas and/or positions get rethought, revisited, extended, and elaborated

Local Revision

- Writing responds to the task productively, although perhaps not comprehensively
- Ideas are developed reasonably well, although perhaps not completely
- Organization is clear, although perhaps may not consistently support ideas and/or thesis
- Argument logic is sound, although it could be bolstered with additional support
- Content is serious and thoughtful
- Writing style, format, and presentation are skillful and appropriate, although would be improved with meticulous revisions

Required Corrections

- ❏ 25–45% rewrite
- ❏ Sentence-level tinkering for precise and elegant expression
- ❏ Word search for most effective diction and turn of phrase
- ❏ Transitional focus to enhance connections between sentences and paragraphs
- ❏ Sections and paragraphs rewritten, rearranged, added, and/or scrapped

Reviewer's Name _____

■ Exercise

Peer Review #12: Peer Review Packet
Looking at a Draft
by Jessica Murray-Cooke

Author Name: _____

Step 1: Thesis Assessment

What is the writer's thesis?—A thesis statement is a narrow, argumentative assertion about a topic which forms the backbone of an essay. It alludes to evidence but does not necessarily "lay it all out" for the reader. The topic has to be questionable, meaning it can be argued. In other words, a thesis statement clearly states the writer's point of view but can still be argued by others. It opens up a debate, rather than shuts one down.

On your peer's paper, underline what you take to be the writer's thesis; then, answer the following questions.

Does the thesis statement directly and clearly answer this assignment prompt question: "Looking at Amir and applying your understanding of Phillips' theory to Amir, how do you assess this character? Is Phillips' work applicable, and more to the point, is the adult Amir a failure or a success?

_____ Yes _____ No

- **If yes,** go to Step 2.

- **If no,** go directly to the draft's closing paragraph. (Often in a draft of an essay, a thesis statement will emerge in a closing paragraph because the writer is finally warmed up and has thought through her ideas.) Is there a budding thesis statement in the closing paragraph that to some degree answers the assignment prompt question above?

_____ Yes _____ No

- **If yes,** underline what you take to be the writer's thesis; then, go to Step 2.

- **If no,** automatically recommend a global revision, a visit to the University Center for Excellence in Writing, and/or a visit with the instructor.

Step 2: Textual Evidence and Analysis Assessment

What is the writer's evidence?—There is a smart and effective three-step method[1] to incorporate quotations into essays that make interpretive arguments.

- **Step One:** Before the writer cites from the literary text, the writer should set up the quotation with her own writing so the reader is not confused about the context of the quotation. (A sophisticated setup can also guide the reader into the writer's interpretation of the passage.)

[1] Adapted from "Using Textual Evidence" by Ben Slote at Allegheny College <webpub.allegheny.edu/dept/writingcenter/assignments/textualevidence.doc> Accessed Sunday, October 21, 2007.

- **Step Two:** Cite the passage. A writer should only quote a passage from the text that illustrates the point in that paragraph.

- **Step Three:** The writer should then follow her selected quotation with writing that analyzes the quotation, explaining how exactly the quotation suggests the point the writer means to make by quoting the passage in the first place and, thus, offers concrete support to the thesis statement.

On your peer's paper, circle every use of direct textual evidence; then, answer the following questions.

In the direct textual evidence circled, does the writer follow the three-step method to incorporate quotations as outlined above?

- **If yes,** indicate on your peer's paper every instance when the writer followed the three-step method and explain how the quoted material helps you understand the writer's thesis.

- **If no,** indicate on your peer's paper every instance when the writer did not follow the three-step method and explain how the quoted material does not help you understand the writer's thesis or why the quotation does not "seem to fit."

Overall, does the writer's selected textual evidence directly and clearly support the writer's thesis statement?

_____ Yes   _____ No

- **If yes,** go to Step 3.

- **If no,** recommend a global revision, a visit to the University Center for Excellence in Writing and/ or a visit with the course instructor.

Step 3: Close Reading, Critical Thinking, Analysis, and Synthesis Evaluation

Directions: Circle the number that best corresponds to your assessment of the writing elements identified below. At the end, tally the total number of points and offer a revision type. Remember, empty praise is just that: empty. If all you do as a reviewer is say, "Nice job!" you haven't really kept up your end of the peer review bargain.

Organization—the order that the ideas are presented in and the logic (or "flow") used to present them

1. Indiscernible, unapparent—I cannot follow this paper's logic and/or order.

2. Unclear and ineffective—I have difficulty following this paper's logic and/or order. I may have a sense of the writer's purpose, but I'm not entirely sure where it's going.

3. Adequate—I'm pretty sure I can follow this paper's logic and/or order. The order and presentation of ideas is competent but not skillful.

4. Capable and proficient—I follow this paper's logic and/or order. The order and presentation of ideas is skillful, but not flawless

5. Successful—I know *exactly* what the writer's stance is and how the writer will argue the case (logic); plus, I know *exactly* where this essay is going (order).

Content—the intrinsic quality or depth of the ideas presented

1. Sketchy, absent, rough, shallow—I neither see nor understand what the writer is trying to say about the texts or how the writer is responding to the task.

2. Vague, imprecise, overly broad—I have difficulty understanding what the writer is trying to say about the texts and/or how the writer is responding to the task.

3. Okay, broad, sometimes unspecific—I can see and understand what the writer is trying to say and how the writer is responding to the task, but I'm not fully convinced by the evidence yet. (This essay demonstrates general understanding of the text and task, though the analysis may not dig in with it fully and the response may not cover the task comprehensively.)

4. Good, interesting, revealing—It is easy to understand what the writer is trying to say and how the writer is responding to the task and working with the texts. (This essay reveals a developed understanding of the text and shows this off by offering thoughtful connections and analysis.)

5. Awesome, rich, dense, thought-provoking, profound—It is effortless to see what the writer is saying and to identify how the writer responds to the task and engages with the texts. (This essay showcases a mature and thorough comprehension of the text and an advanced level of analysis.)

Treatment of Subject—the writer's demonstration of his or her comprehension of the text and the task

1. Novice—I feel like the writer does not understand the texts or the task (or both).

2. Elementary, simple—I feel like the writer needs to re-read the texts and the task.

3. Adequate—I feel like the way the writer wrote about the text and responded to the task provides me just enough material to keep me sustained from start to finish but not enough to make me want to reread it.

4. Skillful—I feel like the way the writer wrote about the texts and responded to the task provides more than enough material to keep me sustained. I may want to reread this essay.

5. Sophisticated—I feel like the way the writer wrote about the text and responded to the task provides loads of material to sustain me; keep me reading and thinking. I definitely want to reread this essay.

Writer's Ethos—the reader's sense of the writer's level of authority over the text and the task

1. Indecisive, fluctuating, inconsistent—I have no idea where the writer stands on the texts and task.

2. Awkward and ambiguous—I have only a vague notion of where the writer stands on the texts and task.

3. Coherent, but not authoritative—I have a good idea where the writer stands on the text and task, but the writer's tone is neither convincing nor authoritative.

4. Convincing, but not necessarily commanding—I am feeling convinced about where the writer stands on the texts and task. This writer seems reasonably sure of herself/himself.

5. Authoritative—I know for sure where this writer stands on the texts and task because the writer is certain of herself/himself (without being overconfident).

Mechanical Errors—issues related to grammar, mechanics, editing, and proofreading

1. More than 12 per page; prohibits readability.

2. More than 5 but fewer than 12 per page; damages readability.

3. More than 5 per page; affects quality of readability, but does not damage it.

4. Fewer than 5 per page; has little to no impact on readability. The writer's style and flair are emerging as interesting elements of her/his writing.

5. Practically flawless; in fact, the writer uses grammar, mechanics, and sentence structure to enhance the work. The writer's style, diction, syntax, and flair are compelling elements of her/his writing.

Information Delivery—the level of the work's "teaching quality"

1. Missing—I didn't learn anything about the texts and the task from this author.

2. Insufficient—I didn't learn anything new about the texts and the task from this author.

3. Thin and commonplace—I learned a little about the texts and the task from this author, but the information presented is probably what most people would say.

4. Substantial in both quantity and quality—I feel like I learned something interesting about the texts and the task from this author. Moreover, the case made is more than what most people would say.

5. Substantial and substantive—I feel significantly taught by this author about the texts and the task. In addition, the case presented is unique, rich, and considerable.

Ideas—the core thinking which lays the foundation for the work overall

1. Shallow and undeveloped; feels like it's been written in haste, without preparation—I feel the writer missed the task and avoided engaging meaningfully with the texts.

2. One-dimensional and underdeveloped—I feel the writer either missed the task or avoided engaging meaningfully with the texts.

3. Straightforward and without expansion and/or maturity—I think the author could do and say more about the texts and the task if the writer builds upon and expands the ideas more.

4. Good quality—I can tell this author has given serious thought to the task and the texts.

5. Exceptional quality—I can see this author has given significant thought to the task and texts.

Second Reading Invitation?

I want to read this paper again because it is interesting, informative, engaging, coherent, cohesive, and educational to me about the text(s).

1. No

2. Yes

Enter Total Score Here: _____ (out of a possible 37)

1 – 14 Global Revision Recommendation

15 – 26 Conceptual Revision Recommendation

27 – 35 Local Revision Recommendation

36 – 37 No Revision Necessary

Three Types of Revisions
Check off your revision type suggestion.

Global Revision
- Writing does not respond to the task
- Ideas are underdeveloped and/or weak and/or biased
- Organization is unclear and/or ineffective
- Argument logic is unsound and/or untraceable
- Content is superficial and/or contains factual errors
- Writing style, format, and presentation are incomplete

Required Corrections
- ❐ Major overhaul of the paper
- ❐ 70–100% rewrite
- ❐ Sections and paragraphs rewritten, rearranged, added, and/or scrapped
- ❐ Retained sections and paragraphs elaborated, qualified, and/or extended

Conceptual Revision

- Writing responds to the task unsuccessfully and/or incompletely
- Ideas show signs of incomplete development
- Organization is ineffective and/or unobvious
- Argument logic is weak and/or biased and/or unrefined
- Content is casual and/or clumsy
- Writing style, format, and presentation are unpolished

Required Corrections
- ❐ Ideas worth keeping and rethinking
- ❐ Prose needs rewriting
- ❐ 45–70% rewrite
- ❐ Crafts a new response to the prompt with the same ideas
- ❐ Sections and paragraphs rewritten, rearranged, added, and/or scrapped
- ❐ Ideas and/or positions get rethought, revisited, extended, and elaborated

Local Revision

- Writing responds to the task productively, although perhaps not comprehensively
- Ideas are developed reasonably well, although perhaps not completely
- Organization is clear, although perhaps may not consistently support ideas and/or thesis
- Argument logic is sound, although it could be bolstered with additional support
- Content is serious and thoughtful
- Writing style, format, and presentation are skillful and appropriate, although would be improved with meticulous revisions

Required Corrections
- ❐ 25–45% rewrite
- ❐ Sentence-level tinkering for precise and elegant expression
- ❐ Word search for most effective diction and turn of phrase
- ❐ Transitional focus to enhance connections between sentences and paragraphs
- ❐ Sections and paragraphs rewritten, rearranged, added, and/or scrapped

Reviewer's Name _____

■ Exercise

Peer Review #12: Peer Review Packet
Looking at a Draft
by Jessica Murray-Cooke

Author Name: _____

Step 1: Thesis Assessment

What is the writer's thesis?—A thesis statement is a narrow, argumentative assertion about a topic which forms the backbone of an essay. It alludes to evidence but does not necessarily "lay it all out" for the reader. The topic has to be questionable, meaning it can be argued. In other words, a thesis statement clearly states the writer's point of view but can still be argued by others. It opens up a debate, rather than shuts one down.

On your peer's paper, underline what you take to be the writer's thesis; then, answer the following questions.

Does the thesis statement directly and clearly answer this assignment prompt question: "Looking at Amir and applying your understanding of Phillips' theory to Amir, how do you assess this character? Is Phillips' work applicable, and more to the point, is the adult Amir a failure or a success?

_____ Yes _____ No

- **If yes,** go to Step 2.

- **If no,** go directly to the draft's closing paragraph. (Often in a draft of an essay, a thesis statement will emerge in a closing paragraph because the writer is finally warmed up and has thought through her ideas.) Is there a budding thesis statement in the closing paragraph that to some degree answers the assignment prompt question above?

_____ Yes _____ No

- **If yes,** underline what you take to be the writer's thesis; then, go to Step 2.

- **If no,** automatically recommend a global revision, a visit to the University Center for Excellence in Writing, and/or a visit with the instructor.

Step 2: Textual Evidence and Analysis Assessment

What is the writer's evidence?—There is a smart and effective three-step method[1] to incorporate quotations into essays that make interpretive arguments.

- **Step One:** Before the writer cites from the literary text, the writer should set up the quotation with her own writing so the reader is not confused about the context of the quotation. (A sophisticated setup can also guide the reader into the writer's interpretation of the passage.)

[1] Adapted from "Using Textual Evidence" by Ben Slote at Allegheny College <webpub.allegheny.edu/dept/writingcenter/ assignments/textualevidence.doc> Accessed Sunday, October 21, 2007.

- **Step Two:** Cite the passage. A writer should only quote a passage from the text that illustrates the point in that paragraph.

- **Step Three:** The writer should then follow her selected quotation with writing that analyzes the quotation, explaining how exactly the quotation suggests the point the writer means to make by quoting the passage in the first place and, thus, offers concrete support to the thesis statement.

On your peer's paper, circle every use of direct textual evidence; then, answer the following questions.

In the direct textual evidence circled, does the writer follow the three-step method to incorporate quotations as outlined above?

- **If yes,** indicate on your peer's paper every instance when the writer followed the three-step method and explain how the quoted material helps you understand the writer's thesis.

- **If no,** indicate on your peer's paper every instance when the writer did not follow the three-step method and explain how the quoted material does not help you understand the writer's thesis or why the quotation does not "seem to fit."

Overall, does the writer's selected textual evidence directly and clearly support the writer's thesis statement?

_____ Yes   _____ No

- **If yes,** go to Step 3.

- **If no,** recommend a global revision, a visit to the University Center for Excellence in Writing and/or a visit with the course instructor.

Step 3: Close Reading, Critical Thinking, Analysis, and Synthesis Evaluation

Directions: Circle the number that best corresponds to your assessment of the writing elements identified below. At the end, tally the total number of points and offer a revision type. Remember, empty praise is just that: empty. If all you do as a reviewer is say, "Nice job!" you haven't really kept up your end of the peer review bargain.

Organization—the order that the ideas are presented in and the logic (or "flow") used to present them

1. Indiscernible, unapparent—I cannot follow this paper's logic and/or order.
2. Unclear and ineffective—I have difficulty following this paper's logic and/or order. I may have a sense of the writer's purpose, but I'm not entirely sure where it's going.
3. Adequate—I'm pretty sure I can follow this paper's logic and/or order. The order and presentation of ideas is competent but not skillful.
4. Capable and proficient—I follow this paper's logic and/or order. The order and presentation of ideas is skillful, but not flawless
5. Successful—I know *exactly* what the writer's stance is and how the writer will argue the case (logic); plus, I know *exactly* where this essay is going (order).

Content—the intrinsic quality or depth of the ideas presented

1. Sketchy, absent, rough, shallow—I neither see nor understand what the writer is trying to say about the texts or how the writer is responding to the task.

2. Vague, imprecise, overly broad—I have difficulty understanding what the writer is trying to say about the texts and/or how the writer is responding to the task.

3. Okay, broad, sometimes unspecific—I can see and understand what the writer is trying to say and how the writer is responding to the task, but I'm not fully convinced by the evidence yet. (This essay demonstrates general understanding of the text and task, though the analysis may not dig in with it fully and the response may not cover the task comprehensively.)

4. Good, interesting, revealing—It is easy to understand what the writer is trying to say and how the writer is responding to the task and working with the texts. (This essay reveals a developed understanding of the text and shows this off by offering thoughtful connections and analysis.)

5. Awesome, rich, dense, thought-provoking, profound—It is effortless to see what the writer is saying and to identify how the writer responds to the task and engages with the texts. (This essay showcases a mature and thorough comprehension of the text and an advanced level of analysis.)

Treatment of Subject—the writer's demonstration of his or her comprehension of the text and the task

1. Novice—I feel like the writer does not understand the texts or the task (or both).

2. Elementary, simple—I feel like the writer needs to re-read the texts and the task.

3. Adequate—I feel like the way the writer wrote about the text and responded to the task provides me just enough material to keep me sustained from start to finish but not enough to make me want to reread it.

4. Skillful—I feel like the way the writer wrote about the texts and responded to the task provides more than enough material to keep me sustained. I may want to reread this essay.

5. Sophisticated—I feel like the way the writer wrote about the text and responded to the task provides loads of material to sustain me; keep me reading and thinking. I definitely want to reread this essay.

Writer's Ethos—the reader's sense of the writer's level of authority over the text and the task

1. Indecisive, fluctuating, inconsistent—I have no idea where the writer stands on the texts and task.

2. Awkward and ambiguous—I have only a vague notion of where the writer stands on the texts and task.

3. Coherent, but not authoritative—I have a good idea where the writer stands on the text and task, but the writer's tone is neither convincing nor authoritative.

4. Convincing, but not necessarily commanding—I am feeling convinced about where the writer stands on the texts and task. This writer seems reasonably sure of herself/himself.

5. Authoritative—I know for sure where this writer stands on the texts and task because the writer is certain of herself/himself (without being overconfident).

Mechanical Errors—issues related to grammar, mechanics, editing, and proofreading

1. More than 12 per page; prohibits readability.

2. More than 5 but fewer than 12 per page; damages readability.

3. More than 5 per page; affects quality of readability, but does not damage it.

4. Fewer than 5 per page; has little to no impact on readability. The writer's style and flair are emerging as interesting elements of her/his writing.

5. Practically flawless; in fact, the writer uses grammar, mechanics, and sentence structure to enhance the work. The writer's style, diction, syntax, and flair are compelling elements of her/his writing.

Information Delivery—the level of the work's "teaching quality"

1. Missing—I didn't learn anything about the texts and the task from this author.

2. Insufficient—I didn't learn anything new about the texts and the task from this author.

3. Thin and commonplace—I learned a little about the texts and the task from this author, but the information presented is probably what most people would say.

4. Substantial in both quantity and quality—I feel like I learned something interesting about the texts and the task from this author. Moreover, the case made is more than what most people would say.

5. Substantial and substantive—I feel significantly taught by this author about the texts and the task. In addition, the case presented is unique, rich, and considerable.

Ideas—the core thinking which lays the foundation for the work overall

1. Shallow and undeveloped; feels like it's been written in haste, without preparation—I feel the writer missed the task and avoided engaging meaningfully with the texts.

2. One-dimensional and underdeveloped—I feel the writer either missed the task or avoided engaging meaningfully with the texts.

3. Straightforward and without expansion and/or maturity—I think the author could do and say more about the texts and the task if the writer builds upon and expands the ideas more.

4. Good quality—I can tell this author has given serious thought to the task and the texts.

5. Exceptional quality—I can see this author has given significant thought to the task and texts.

Second Reading Invitation?

I want to read this paper again because it is interesting, informative, engaging, coherent, cohesive, and educational to me about the text(s).

1. No

2. Yes

Enter Total Score Here: _____ (out of a possible 37)

1 – 14 Global Revision Recommendation

15 – 26 Conceptual Revision Recommendation

27 – 35 Local Revision Recommendation

36 – 37 No Revision Necessary

Three Types of Revisions

Check off your revision type suggestion.

Global Revision

- Writing does not respond to the task
- Ideas are underdeveloped and/or weak and/or biased
- Organization is unclear and/or ineffective
- Argument logic is unsound and/or untraceable
- Content is superficial and/or contains factual errors
- Writing style, format, and presentation are incomplete

Required Corrections

- ❒ Major overhaul of the paper
- ❒ 70–100% rewrite
- ❒ Sections and paragraphs rewritten, rearranged, added, and/or scrapped
- ❒ Retained sections and paragraphs elaborated, qualified, and/or extended

Conceptual Revision

- Writing responds to the task unsuccessfully and/or incompletely
- Ideas show signs of incomplete development
- Organization is ineffective and/or unobvious
- Argument logic is weak and/or biased and/or unrefined
- Content is casual and/or clumsy
- Writing style, format, and presentation are unpolished

Required Corrections

- ☐ Ideas worth keeping and rethinking
- ☐ Prose needs rewriting
- ☐ 45–70% rewrite
- ☐ Crafts a new response to the prompt with the same ideas
- ☐ Sections and paragraphs rewritten, rearranged, added, and/or scrapped
- ☐ Ideas and/or positions get rethought, revisited, extended, and elaborated

Local Revision

- Writing responds to the task productively, although perhaps not comprehensively
- Ideas are developed reasonably well, although perhaps not completely
- Organization is clear, although perhaps may not consistently support ideas and/or thesis
- Argument logic is sound, although it could be bolstered with additional support
- Content is serious and thoughtful
- Writing style, format, and presentation are skillful and appropriate, although would be improved with meticulous revisions

Required Corrections

- ☐ 25–45% rewrite
- ☐ Sentence-level tinkering for precise and elegant expression
- ☐ Word search for most effective diction and turn of phrase
- ☐ Transitional focus to enhance connections between sentences and paragraphs
- ☐ Sections and paragraphs rewritten, rearranged, added, and/or scrapped

GRAMMAR/LANGUAGE/FORMATTING

Name _____

■ Exercise

Error Sheet Sample and Forms

by Jessica Murray-Cooke

© copyright 2008. Used with permission.

In this column, write the sentence that contains the sentence-level error from your essay. (Circle) the error.	In this column, cite the page and the rule or guideline from the grammar manual. Note: if the manual's language is too clunky, rewrite the rule in your own language.	In this column, rewrite the sentence that contains the sentence-level error in your essay. Correct the error, and (circle) the correction.
Ex. When Rosaldo studied the Ilongot tribe and their bereavement (rituals; he) came up with different reasons for why they would head-hunt as a form of relief for grief but was wrong every time.	Ex. Page 268—Setting off Introductory Elements. "An introductory dependent clause is generally set off from the rest of the sentence by a comma" (Kirszner 268).	Ex. When Rosaldo studied the Ilongot tribe and their bereavement (rituals, he) came up with different reasons for why they would head-hunt as a form of relief for grief but was wrong every time.
Ex. The long drive in our little blue Sentra was anything but bearable, (this) was nothing compared to the living arrangements that took place once we got there.	Ex. Page 276—Editing Misused Commas. "A comma alone cannot be used to join two independent clauses; it must be followed by a coordinating conjunction. Using just a comma to connect two independent clauses creates a comma splice" (Kirszner 276).	Ex. The long drive in our little blue Sentra was anything but bearable, (yet) this was nothing compared to the living arrangements that took place once we got there.
Ex. Renato Rosaldo proposes his re-positioning in understanding the Ilongot culture and their head-hunting (ritual's) after facing the death of his wife.	Ex. Page 28—Editing Misused Apostrophes. "Do not use apostrophes with plural nouns that are not posses-sive" (Kirszner 287).	Ex. Renato Rosaldo proposes his re-positioning in understanding the Ilongot culture and their head-hunting (rituals) after facing the death of his wife.

In this column, write the sentence that contains the sentence-level error from your essay. (Circle) the error.	In this column, cite the page and the rule or guideline from the grammar manual. Note: if the manual's language is too clunky, rewrite the rule in your own language.	In this column, rewrite the sentence that contains the sentence-level error in your essay. Correct the error, and (circle) the correction.

Name _____

In this column, write the sentence that contains the sentence-level error from your essay. (Circle) the error.	In this column, cite the page and the rule or guideline from the grammar manual. Note: if the manual's language is too clunky, rewrite the rule in your own language.	In this column, rewrite the sentence that contains the sentence-level error in your essay. Correct the error, and (circle) the correction.

Name _____

In this column, write the sentence that contains the sentence-level error from your essay. (Circle) the error.	In this column, cite the page and the rule or guideline from the grammar manual. Note: if the manual's language is too clunky, rewrite the rule in your own language.	In this column, rewrite the sentence that contains the sentence-level error in your essay. Correct the error, and (circle) the correction.

Name _____

In this column, write the sentence that contains the sentence-level error from your essay. Circle the error.	In this column, cite the page and the rule or guideline from the grammar manual. Note: if the manual's language is too clunky, rewrite the rule in your own language.	In this column, rewrite the sentence that contains the sentence-level error in your essay. Correct the error, and circle the correction.

Name _____

In this column, write the sentence that contains the sentence-level error from your essay. (Circle) the error.	In this column, cite the page and the rule or guideline from the grammar manual. Note: if the manual's language is too clunky, rewrite the rule in your own language.	In this column, rewrite the sentence that contains the sentence-level error in your essay. Correct the error, and (circle) the correction.

Name _____

In this column, write the sentence that contains the sentence-level error from your essay. (Circle) the error.	In this column, cite the page and the rule or guideline from the grammar manual. Note: if the manual's language is too clunky, rewrite the rule in your own language.	In this column, rewrite the sentence that contains the sentence-level error in your essay. Correct the error, and (circle) the correction.

Draft Checklist

I. Formal Concerns

Heading
✓ Do you have all four elements?

✓ Is the heading in the upper left-hand corner of the first page?

✓ Is it double-spaced?

✓ Is the date in the correct format (ex: 27 February 2007)?

✓ Do you use correct and proper capitalization?

✓ Did you spell your instructor's name correctly?

Header
✓ Is it in the proper form (ex: Lopez 1)?

✓ Is it in the upper right-hand corner of every page, including the first?

Title
✓ Do you have a title that reflects the argument of your paper?

✓ Do you omit all punctuation and emphasis, such as italics, underlining, or bold?

✓ Is the title in the same font as the rest of the paper?

✓ Is it centered?

✓ Is it in the correct location, immediately after the heading, immediately before the first paragraph?

Spacing
✓ Have you made sure that you do not skip extra lines before or after the title (beyond the normal double-spacing)?

✓ Have you made sure that you do not skip lines between paragraphs?

Margins
✓ Are margins one inch on all sides, all pages?

Essay titles
✓ Do you have the correct, full title of the essay when you first mention it?

✓ Are you using the correct punctuation (underlining/italics for books, quotation marks for chapters, introductions, epilogues, and essays)?

Quotation
✓ Are you using proper parenthetical notation?

✓ Are you remembering where to put the period, comma, or other punctuation?

✓ Are you using block quotations properly (for quotations longer than four typed lines)?

✓ Are you using correct block quotation form?

✓ Are you correctly citing indirect sources?

✓ Are your quotes accurately typed?

✓ Have you remembered to give notation for every quotation?

II. Stylistic Matters

Introduction
✓ Do you introduce the full name of every author you will address in the paper?

✓ Do you introduce the full, correct name of every book or essay you address in the paper?

✓ Do you remember to introduce your argument, making it clearly stated?

✓ Is your introduction too long or too short?

Transitions
✓ Do you make a smooth transition between every paragraph in your paper?

Questions
✓ Have you turned questions into statements to make your point more strongly?

Paragraphs
✓ Do you break apart any paragraphs that last more than one entire page?

✓ Do you have any paragraphs that seem to be too short?

Tone
✓ Have you managed to make your argument without belittling any author?

✓ Have you remained respectful of all authors while making your point?

✓ Have you sounded condescending or dismissive of any author?

III. Content

Balance
✓ Do you devote too much time and space to one author?

✓ Do you devote too little time and space to one author?

✓ Is the space you devote to each author just enough to illustrate your argument?

✓ Is there any section you could condense in order to move more quickly to your argument?

✓ Is there any section you could expand to better illustrate the argument you are making?

Argument
✓ Is the majority of your paper your argument, not a summary of each author's position?

✓ Do you illustrate your argument using quotation?

✓ Have you proven your argument?

Bibliography
✓ Is your bibliography on a separate page?

✓ Do you have "Bibliography" or "Works Cited" centered at the top of that page?

✓ Do you double space all entries without making extra spaces between entries?

✓ Do you alphabetize all entries?

✓ Do you use correct bibliographic form?